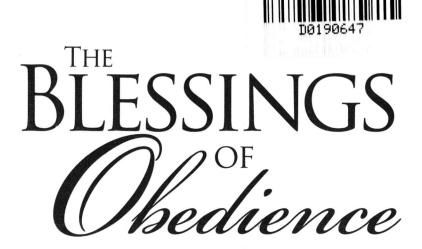

THE
BLESSINGS
OF
Obedience

OUR STORY OF
HOW GOD HAS
LED AND BLESSED
OUR FAMILY

BOB FRALEY

Copyright 2010
Robert R. Fraley
All rights reserved
ISBN 978-0-615-40688-6

Published by
Christian Life Outreach
P.O. Box 31129
Phoenix, Arizona 85046-1129
Phone: 866-998-4136
E-mail: xnlifeout@yahoo.com
Website: www.bobfraleychristianlifeoutreach.com

Printed in the United States of America

Design by Robin Black, www.blackbirdcreative.biz

ACKNOWLEDGMENT

I wish to acknowledge all of our children
and their spouses: Dave & Marilyn Parks,
Larry & Susan Mitchell, Bud & Brenda Allison,
Mary Mitchell, Perry & Teresa Fraley,
Robert & Andrea VanHofwegen,
Shawn & Alice O'Shell, Greg & Gina Fraley,
and Michael & Heather Fraley along with their families for their continued faithfulness
in serving the Lord.

CONTENTS

Preface 7

1. God Will Take Care of Us 9

2. Early Years 13

3. The Lord Adds To Our Family 23

4. A Revolutionary Encounter With God 31

5. The Event That Changed America Forever.....49

6. My Noah Experience......................................63

7. Three Tests..69

8. Preparation For A Move 79

9. The Move..87

10. The Lord Continues to Lead 95

11. 1974 To 1980 105

12. 1980 To 1995 115

13. 1995 To 2000..121

14. A Look At Fruit...141

15. My Last Major Calling..................................163

16. Building Your Family's Spiritual Ark 175

Epilogue...191

Appendix A 197

PREFACE

For Bob and Barbara Fraley, Saturday, October 4, 1969 produced an experience similar to Noah and his call to build an ark for the saving of his family. Just as God spoke to Noah and gave him a unique assignment, so too, did God speak, first to Bob, then to Barbara. On that October day, the Fraley's God-given assignment was to add six children to their existing two children. Overnight, in their early thirties they now had eight children that ranged in age from two to eighteen to nurture and love.

The story of what happened on that October day and what has transpired over the last forty years as God has led them in building an ark—not physical like Noah but spiritual—for the saving of their family in these last days is an amazing and powerful story of remarkable courage, moral resolve and what it means to live a practical life of faith and trust in God, when to do so appeared to be contrary to all human reason and logic.

Bob writes as he has lived. Their story is about how God can take two ordinary lives and create an extraordinary and transforming experience that has changed the lives of not only two families, but a countless number of people. It is a story of divine revelation, transformational life choices, miraculous guidance and provision of how God led Bob and his wife to move their family across the country, establish and participate in Christian Schools, help build two very successful businesses, found Christian Life

Outreach through which they developed; a Christian Retreat Center, a missionary outreach in Kenya, East Africa, a Christian publishing outreach of books, booklets, and newsletters, a "Campaign to Save Christian Values in America," and a ministry to help other parents build their "spiritual ark" for the saving of their family in these last days.

By every description the life of Bob and Barbara Fraley is a living demonstration of God's grace and mercy to a family and a nation. This then is an inspirational story and an example of what a person and a family can accomplish when God is at the center of everything they do and think. It's also the story of a man who continued to hear God's still small voice.

DERALD McDANIEL
Executive Director of Christian Life Outreach
& Bob and Barbara's Former Pastor

HUGH STEVEN
Wycliffe Bible Translators

ONE

GOD'S GOING TO TAKE CARE OF US

That October 4, 1969 Saturday morning in northeastern Ohio, was the kind of day that lived-up to the State's motto, A Great Place to Live and Work. The autumn air was clean, crisp and invigorating. The bright slanting sun had burned off a light skiff of early morning frost. The corn fields were turning golden yellow and leaves on the maple trees were in a riot of multicolor—oranges, reds and browns.

Seventeen-year-old Larry Mitchell was up early on this Saturday morning. For added income, he and his father Roland had started a small tire business, and Larry was excited to be delivering four new tires he had sold to a new customer.

Larry's father, Roland, and his mother, Eugie and the six children (five girls and a boy) had, after six years of living in the basement of the home he was building in his spare time, recently moved into their completed home.

Roland, an electrician, worked the swing shift at the local General Electric plant. Larry knew his father had to be back home by 1:00 p.m. when a co-worker would pick him up and drive to the plant.

It was Saturday and the kids had slept late. After breakfast, Larry loaded the four tires into the family's 1965 Chevy station wagon and was urging everyone to "get this show on the road." At the last moment, Larry's mother Eugie decided that since it was such a beautiful fall day, she would go along for the ride. And not to be left out of the excitement, ten-year-old Andrea and four-year-old Alice begged their parents to let them go as well. Finally, at about 10:30, Larry got those going along settled in the station wagon and, with Roland driving, pulled out of their driveway at R.R. #1 Petersburg, Ohio.

The country road to Larry's client took them through an area of large fields of standing corn that ran almost to either side of the road forming a kind of golden corridor. Then about seven minutes into their trip, in the blink of an eye, the warmth of their family togetherness turned into the most searing and painful of human tragedies. Without warning, a farmer in his pickup truck, blinded by the cornfield that ran to the corner of the intersection, failed to stop and crashed directly into the driver's side of the Mitchell's 1965 station wagon. Roland was killed instantly. The pickup struck the station wagon with such force that it slammed the vehicle into a tree on the opposite side of the road. The impact knocked Eugie unconscious as it did Andrea and Alice. Larry, his sisters and his mother were rushed twenty miles to the hospital in New Castle, Pennsylvania. Tragically, Eugie Mitchell died later that day. She was forty-two. Larry, like the man in the pickup truck, escaped with just a few bruises and scratches as did the man's two children who were also in the truck.

Mitchell's two other children, fifteen-year-old Brenda, and thirteen-year-old Mary, had remained at home. The Mitchell's eldest daughter Marilyn, age eighteen, was in her freshman year at a small college in Parkersburg, West Virginia, just thirty-five miles from where her grandparents lived. One of the elders from where the Mitchell's attended church broke the news to Marilyn. Three ladies from the church came to the house to tell Brenda and Mary.

The trauma of the accident soon engulfed the sensibilities of the entire community, but none more than the children. When Roland's co-worker, unaware of what had happened, drove by to pick him up, he found Brenda sitting on the front lawn. When the co-worker asked about her father, all Brenda could say was, "My dad's not going to work today." It fell to the ladies from the Mitchell's church to explain what had happened. They had decided to stay with Brenda and Mary the rest of the day.

Two days after the accident, Larry was released from the hospital and immediately began to help plan his parent's funeral. On the day of the funeral, friends offered their sincere consolations and expressed their desire to help Larry and his sisters in any way they could. After the reception, a small group of friends remained behind to offer Larry and his sisters' further consolation. During the conversation, someone asked Larry, "What are you and your sisters going to do now?" Without a moment's hesitation, Larry said, "I don't know, but God is going to take care of us."

Who can know what was in Larry's mind and heart at that moment, except that in the midst of a pointless tragedy that was beyond his control, his horizon was on God, not on despair. Thus, unknowingly, Larry was able to speak some prophetic words unaware of what the Lord had spoken to me and my wife, Barbara, the night of the accident that would change the children's lives and our lives forever.

On the day of the accident, Barbara and I left town early to visit friends in Detroit, Michigan, about a four-hour drive from our home. We had planned to stay overnight and return Sunday evening. However, as Saturday evening approached, we both sensed we should return home. Not really understanding why, we packed and arrived back home at about eleven p.m. Our first order of business was to pick up our eleven-year-old son Perry who had stayed with our minister's family for the weekend. Our two year old son Greg had stayed with a neighbor.

I'll forever remember the surprise on our minister's face when he saw me standing at his front door. "Bob," he said, "We weren't expecting you until Sunday. You must have heard about the accident." I said, "No, I haven't heard about an accident." And then he told me the tragic news. "Roland Mitchell (one of our church elders) and his wife Eugie were both killed in an automobile accident this morning about eleven o'clock. Their three children, Larry, Andrea and Alice, were with them in the car. At last report the children are still alive, however, Alice is in critical condition and Andrea may not live. Larry is going to be okay."

When I heard this news and told Barbara, it was as if someone had stabbed us in the heart, and we both broke down in tears. After I learned the children were in the hospital in New Castle, and even though we didn't know the family well and it was approaching midnight, I felt I should immediately drive the twenty miles to the hospital. My visit was to be a never-to-be-forgotten experience.

TWO

THE EARLY YEARS

B efore I tell you how profoundly that midnight visit to the hospital affected our lives, let me tell you a little about ourselves. Barbara and I were both raised on farms in the southwestern part of Ohio. Barbara had two brothers one older and one younger and a sister three years her senior. Her parent's farm was just a few miles from my parent's hundred acre farm.

I was the youngest of thirteen children. Charles, my older brother by two years, was to have a major impact on my life (more about this later). Both my parents were seriously committed to the Lord Jesus Christ. People who knew my mother, testified she lived an exemplary Christian life, much like the outstanding godly women of the Bible.

I made my own commitment to the Lord during a small farm-town revival meeting at age nine. I remember being baptized in a muddy creek that cut through our farm. Barbara also made her own commitment to faith in Jesus Christ at an early age.

Growing up on my father's Ohio farm followed a time-honored tradition of finishing our chores before breakfast, and in time for school. My mother always prepared a hardy, warm farm breakfast. One of my favorite chores, morning and late afternoon—except winter—was to walk through our pasture fields to round up our grazing cows and bring them into the barn for milking. This took about twenty to thirty minutes and I used the time to pray and sing praises to the Lord. Since my father could not afford the luxury of milking machines, all of my brothers and sisters who were at home had milking responsibilities. I milked my first cow when I was ten.

Our local high school was in Hollansburg, Ohio, about a mile from our home. The movie, *Hoosiers*, was a kind of reenactment of our athletic program. During high school, basketball was king. I was good enough to receive county and state honors in basketball which led to my being recruited by several small Ohio universities. Barbara was also an excellent athlete. However, during her high school years at Hollansburg, the athletic program for girls had been discontinued. Not to be left out of her high school extracurricular activities, Barbara became a cheerleader and drum majorette.

After graduating from high school, and to preempt the draft law still in effect in the forties and early fifties, my brothers Charles and Kirby had joined the Navy. When it came time for me to graduate, my father said, "Two of my sons in the military are enough. I want you to go to college." Capital University in Columbus, Ohio, was the Alma Mater of my high school coach, and at his urging I enrolled there. My farm chores had made me strong, and since I was the fastest kid on our high school track team, I decided to try out for football; a sport we did not have at our small high school.

I soon learned, however, that I wasn't as strong as I thought I was. The fall of my freshman year was exceptionally dry, which made the playing field at Capital exceptionally hard. Running in cleats was a new experience for me, and the repeated practice runs gave me severe shin splints, and for many weeks I could not walk but a few steps at a time on concrete or a hard surface. This, of course, disqualified me from playing football or basketball.

Determined not to be defeated by this turn of events, I fell back on yet another of my interests, singing. In high school I had won a singing competition and decided to try out for the men's glee club. Happily, I was selected and soon discovered that the Capital University's men's glee club was an elite group that was invited to travel and put on concerts throughout the eastern U.S. My shin splint misfortune turned me in another direction and opened a window of opportunity that proved to be one of the most enjoyable experiences of my freshman college experience.

Since my parents had only been able to help financially with my first year of college, I decided to transfer to a less expensive state school. Miami University, Oxford, Ohio was just forty miles from home and it had a basketball team that I was anxious to join. The several days I tried out as a walk-on during tryouts, the head coach was ill. In his stead, the assistant coach selected me for the team. When the head coach returned several days later, he called me into his office and said, "Bob I'm sorry, but I am going to have to make a change. We have a young man who is 6'5" and played for a large school in Columbus. Since you are 5'9 ½" I am going to have to go with him. I know this is a hard blow for you. You are a great fellow, I like you, and you have been the top scorer in the tryouts, but the reality is, I have to go with the taller man."

Coming from a small farm school, and believing I had made a major university basketball team, made me feel like I was sitting on top of the world. What a few days earlier had been one of the happiest days of my life was now one of the saddest. Being cut was not only one of the hardest things I had ever experienced, it wiped out any chance of my receiving an athletic scholarship. I

was now on my own to work my way through the next three years
of college, which I did.

For some, being away from home in a fun-loving atmosphere
free from parental restrictions can be a dangerous time for a nine-
teen-year-old farm boy. Outwardly I was the model of a good citi-
zen; I wasn't into drugs or alcohol. Yet my life began to reflect the
spiritual truth of I Corinthians 15:33 (RSV), *"Do not be deceived,
bad company ruins good morals."* And I was often in bad company
to the extent that I stopped attending church or fellowshipping
with other Christian believers.

Barbara was still in high school when I was at Miami University. After graduating from high school in 1955, she attended
cosmetology school and worked in Richmond, Indiana. We had
never dated but knew each other as she and my niece were best of
friends and would often visit my mother.

It was during the summer of 1956 that we first dated while I
was home from college. How does one describe the girl you fall in
love with? The best description I know is that whenever she enters
a room, it lights up. She is not only pretty; she has the vivacious
witty energy of Barbara Streisand as in the movie *Hello Dolly*. And
she also possesses a warm, honest magic charm that draws children to her as Maria did in *The Sound of Music*. Additionally she
has a natural athletic ability. She would regularly trounce me in
bowling, and even when I became a good golfer, Barbara would,
if I wasn't careful, come close to beating me even though she only
played a few times a year.

Her personality and wit turns almost any activity into an
exciting fun time for everyone. To illustrate I'll site a couple of
examples out of hundreds throughout our marriage. One evening
she said, "Let's all go to the ice cream parlor for banana splits."
We soon piled into the car and were on our way. We were seated

and began to give the waitress our order for banana splits when the waitress said, "We are out of bananas." Barbara replied, "But that is one of your specialties, how could you be out of bananas?" She knew it wasn't the fault of the waitress, but rather than ordering something else, she got up and said, "Let's go." While driving away and passing a nearby grocery store she asked me to pull in. She got out and went in the store, returning in a few minutes with her arms full of bananas and said, "Let's go back to the ice cream parlor." As the family went in smiling, she handed the hostess the bananas and with a chuckle asked if we could now order banana splits. She said, "There are even plenty for several other customers." She was a big hit with the help, other customers, the kids and we had our banana splits.

Disneyland in Orlando, Florida opened the fall of 1971. The summer of 1972 we decided to take the family there for our vacation. It was a long two day trip to Florida and during the second day with a packed car the kids were getting restless. Barbara asked me to exit the interstate and drive along the country roads to take in some of the local color. We drove by an old farm house near the road and sitting out front under a shade tree was an elderly gentleman next to a table full of watermelons. Barbara said, "Stop and go back." We all got out and she chose a forty pound watermelon and cut it up. It had just been picked that day and was as red and sweet as any melon I ever tasted. The family sat there with this elderly man and we ate the whole melon. That was an event our kids remember to this day.

I graduated from Miami University in January, 1957. Immediately upon graduating I went to work for an insurance company and was assigned to represent them at the University of Maryland campus. One of the conditions for accepting this job was I had to move to Washington, D.C. Three months later, I returned from

D.C. for our wedding as Barbara and I had set the date for late April. We started our married life together in D.C. in a happy state of marital bliss when four months after our arrival our lives were sadly interrupted. I joined the Air Force Reserves, knowing if I didn't I would be drafted into the Army. I had to "pay the piper" by leaving for active duty.

I was away on active duty for the next six months. Afterward, I was required to attend one weekend a month and two weeks each summer in active training. I did this for the next five and a half years. Since my tour of duty was just six months, it allowed me to continue my career opportunities and Barbara and I could be together.

My major at Miami had been in mathematics and pre-engineering (Miami did not have a complete engineering department). While I was grateful for my job with the insurance company (it taught me a lot about sales and marketing), I soon realized this was not going to be my long-term career. I needed a greater technical challenge and responded to open positions with IBM and General Electric. Ultimately, however, in late 1958 I accepted a position with Reynolds Aluminum in their Cincinnati industrial sales division.

I was now on my way to achieving the American Dream of a successful business career with all the amenities. However, as Barbara and I molded our lives together, I slowly but surely began drawing her away from many of her early Christian values. I developed the habit of social drinking, I had taken up smoking and I wasn't averse to using a well-placed expletive. For almost the decade of our twenties we lived with little or no thought of a committed Christian life.

And then at age twenty-nine, something of my earlier Christian teaching began to stir in my heart and mind. In a rather pragmatic fashion, I reasoned that if I had been diligent enough to work and put myself through college in order to have a successful forty-or fifty-year career, it only made sense to learn more about eternal things. In addition, I began to think more seriously about the future and influence I was having on our first-born son Perry who was born a year after our marriage.

This motivated me to begin a serious and thoughtful reading of the Bible. With the truths of God's Word occupying my mind and asking God in prayer for direction and understanding, Barbara and I recommitted our lives to the Lord Jesus Christ. It happened during a revival meeting at the church we had started attending. As I look back more than forty-five years after that event, I marvel at the way God worked in our lives during that moment in time.

My first Sunday experience at that church, which was to become our church home, was unique. Barbara was sick with measles and stayed home. Perry age six and I went by ourselves and took a pew at the back of the church so that we could make a quick exit. At the conclusion of the service, and before the rest of the congregation could exit the sanctuary, an elder beat me to the door. When the elder shook my hand he said, "Would you please stand here beside me and meet some of the people as they come out." Years later, this elder, who had become a good friend and was at the time chair of the elder's board, told me he had never before or since that Sunday ever asked a new person to stand with him at the door to meet the people. He said, "For some reason I just felt led to do that."

After recommitting our lives to the Lord, the minister and elders wanted Barbara and me to be rebaptized. Since I had already been baptized I questioned the reason for their request. But we also had a strong desire to be obedient for whatever the Lord wanted us to do, and both Barbara and I agreed to the elders request.

Though that was nearly 45 years ago, I remember the night we were baptized like it was yesterday. I am sure one of the reasons is because in college I had picked up the habit of smoking, social drinking and on occasion using a curse word. The night I came out of the waters of baptism something miraculous happened. I really don't know how to explain it, but my baptism experience completely delivered me from the addiction of cigarettes, from ever wanting any kind of alcoholic drink to again touch my lips, and all my words immediately became pure, never even uttering the "d" word since that day. I cannot take any credit for this. This change happened, not by my power or strength, but by the Spirit of God! Additionally, serving the Lord became the center of our activities and has remained so up to the present.

During the years I worked for Reynolds Aluminum my career advanced rapidly. I received the company's top industrial sales award and was appointed District Sales Manager of their Youngstown, Ohio sales office. At age thirty-two I was recruited by Benada Aluminum and accepted the position as Vice President and General Manager. Benada Aluminum, a manufacturing company that produces aluminum extrusions was located in a suburb of Youngstown, and was one of Reynolds, as well as my largest customers.

I have often thought that our popular culture has presented a false assumption about how to be successful in business. The owner of the Benada Company was Jewish. When I went to work for him he knew of my commitment to serve the Lord and told me he respected my commitment. Not only that, but when I interviewed for the job, I told him frankly I didn't know how to run a company, which was what I was being hired to do. He said, "Do not worry about that! I am more interested in someone I can trust. It is your faith commitment that leads me to believe I can

THE BLESSINGS OF OBEDIENCE

trust you. What I need is someone who is teachable, and I will teach you how to run the business." And that, in fact, is what he did. I was happy to be working with one of the most successful individuals in this business.

The first few years of our recommitment to serve the Lord passed quickly. Nine and half years after Perry was born, our second child, Greg, was born. We purchased fifteen acres of land near the community where we lived and began thinking about building our dream house. With my business career becoming well-established and our family life centered on church activities, everything in our family was coming together nicely. We were busy raising our two boys, working at my career, and serving the Lord. I became a Bible teacher, and was appointed a deacon and we became active in evangelism. Barbara was known as "Mrs. Energy" because she was able to accomplish so much in a day. Her boundless gift of hospitality along with her personality was put to full use by the Lord. It would be difficult to count the number of times we had from 25 to 150 people in our home for a sit-down dinner, served hot and fresh, complete with decorations.

Her gift of hospitality was a blessing and a joy that the Spirit of God used to minister comfort and peace in a heart-warming atmosphere of love and tranquility to all who came to our table. Often, after a dinner party, our visitors would say they just didn't want to leave. Barbara's wit and her gift to cheer came straight out of Proverbs 17:22 that says, *"A cheerful heart is good medicine."*

The accident that claimed the life of Roland and Eugie Mitchell occurred about five years after our recommitment to the Lord. Unknown to Barbara and me, that day would forever change everything in our lives beyond our wildest imagination.

THREE

THE LORD ADDS TO OUR FAMILY

After our minister told us about the tragedy that took the lives of Roland and Eugie Mitchell, I took Barbara and Perry home and left immediately for the hospital. When I arrived, I discovered ten-year Andrea had a fractured skull with such severe brain damage she was pronounced hopeless. Hospital staff had decided to leave the usual patient-cleanup procedure to the mortuary. Four-year-old Alice was on the critical list but appeared to be okay. Seventeen-year-old Larry had escaped with only minor cuts and bruises.

As I drove home from the hospital in the early hours of that Sunday morning, I had an extraordinary experience with the Lord. For the first time in my life, I felt the Lord speaking directly to me. There was no audible voice, but what I heard in my heart was clearly and unmistakably divine. The Lord said: "Build a new house on the land you recently bought and take these six orphaned children to raise." The voice in my mind and heart was so clear I knew it was a direct word from the Lord.

However, the problem I pondered all the way home was, how am I going to share this revelation with Barbara? I knew to be obedient to this word from the Lord would forever change our lives.

The responsibility would be huge. Not only that, the burden would be greater on Barbara than it would be on me and what about our own children? Our second son, Greg, was too young to understand the implications, but-eleven-year old Perry would now have to share our attention, normally given exclusively to him, with six other children.

Barbara has always had an enormous heart for people. And when I told her what I had experienced from the Lord, she amazed me by saying she too felt this was a message from God and that we should be obedient to His call. At the same time, the thought of assuming the care and responsibility for six more children, four of whom were teenagers, seemed completely overwhelming and even a little frightening. But as we began to pray about this, the Lord gave us a sense of peace and the confidence that He would supply all we would need to carry out this new responsibility in His name.

The next act of God intervening in the children's welfare after the word I received coming home from the hospital was with Andrea's injuries. I stated earlier that Andrea was in critical condition, so much so the hospital personnel had given up hope of her ever recovering. But then the Christian community began to pray specifically for her. And beyond all expectations Andrea lived through the first night. She was then transferred to a hospital closer to home. The next morning in church I was asked to lead a congregational prayer for the family and especially for Andrea. As I was praying, I felt a quickening in my spirit. It brought a certain faith to believe Andrea was going to be healed.

However, the doctors at the hospital, where Andrea had been moved had an opposite view. In order to save her life the doctors said she needed immediate surgery to remove the pressure from her brain. They also said that even if the procedure was successful and Andrea lived, she would be unable to return to school until the following fall—eleven months away. Even then, they warned, she may never make a complete recovery and would in all probability be a physical and mental invalid for the rest of her life.

But unknown to these competent physicians, God had another option for Andrea. In answer to the many fervent payers, the Lord completely healed Andrea's damaged brain. Remarkably, the surgeons never had a chance to operate. Within three weeks she was back in school full of life and vigor. There was yet another beautiful thing the Lord did for Andrea. Born with a malfunctioning kidney, she had been a sickly child who required twice daily medication and was continuously under a doctor's care. At age ten she weighed only forty-one pounds, the normal weight of a four or five year-old.

Remarkably when the Lord healed Andrea's head injuries, He also healed her dysfunctional kidney. Kidney medicine and frequent visits to the doctor became a thing of the past. Within a year her weight doubled to eighty-two pounds. She blossomed from a frail, sickly child to a strong, robust child. Today, Andrea and her husband have four grown boys and own and operate a large dairy farm near Phoenix, Arizona.

Only a few days had passed after the accident when Barbara and I felt we should let it be known that we would take the children into our home. However, doing God's will, as His servants have experienced down through the centuries, often comes with unexpected trials, snags and barriers. Our first roadblock was from family and friends who reminded us about how busy we were with home, church and work. "You don't need such an added responsibility in your lives," they said. "Everything is so perfect in your home. You have so much going for you." They also reminded us we were only in our early thirties with most of our marriage and family life ahead of us.

In many respects, their objections were legitimate. Our lives were rich, full and we were happily contented. We truly were not looking for additional work to do for the Lord. Nor were we overly altruistic. But, of course, the Lord had spoken to us, not to them. Barbara and I were also challenged by the promise in John 15:16 where Jesus said, *"You did not choose me, but I chose you and appointed you to go and bear fruit—fruit that will last. Then the Father will give you whatever you ask in my name."* We firmly believed God had chosen us for this task.

The next difficultly was a legal one. Since the children's parents hadn't left a will, the disposition of the children was in the hands of the court. At first nothing seemed to be in our favor. We had never met any of the children's relatives. They all strongly objected to our parenting them. Still, we made it known to the probate judge we were eager to take the children. Meanwhile, some of the relatives tried to convince the judge to have the children live with them. Yet with the crack of his gavel the state probate judge appointed us their legal guardians. We were never told why. All he said was, "This is the decision I have made." We knew of no other explanation except that it was indeed the hand of the Lord. In that moment, our new family became a reality just as the Lord had directed through His word while I drove home from the hospital that night after the accident.

Solving legal problems was just the beginning of the Lord's interventions on our behalf. We had obeyed part one of the Lord's command, "Take these children to raise," but there was another part: "Build a new house on the land you recently bought." At the time of the accident, we lived in a three-bedroom, single bath house. Now, as the parents of eight children (making a total of ten in our household), we became acutely aware we needed a larger house.

For some time, Barbara had been leisurely looking at house plans in anticipation of building our dream house on our newly-acquired acreage. However, time was now of the essence, and we quickly decided on a final set of house plans, found a general contractor, and signed a contract. Then we ran into a major problem! In order to have sufficient funds to finish the new house we not only needed a bank loan, we also needed the equity we had in our current house. Once again, the hand of God intervened on our behalf. Before we listed our house with a realtor, a man who was aware our house was for sale astonished us by agreeing to buy our house, pay our asking price, and he and his wife <u>paid us cash in advance</u>. Further, knowing it would take several months before we could take possession of our new home, he said, "Live in your current home for as long as it takes to complete your new house." This was unheard of! But, it was exactly what we needed to get the equity out of our old house. We were amazed and thanked the Lord for His faithfulness.

This became an exciting time for the family. We met with the builder, visited the construction site every day or two and watched the house take shape. Barbara shared with each of the children the location of their rooms and talked about how they would decorate it.

One of the plans we had for every room was for them to be wired with speakers so we could play Christian music. We made a commitment to play only Christian music in place of the often less edifying secular music. That may sound like we were old prudes, but we believed we were being obedient to God's Word that instructs us to meditate on His Word morning, noon and night.

By the time the ten of us had settled into our new home (our youngest son Michael had not yet been born), it was evident the Lord had used the construction of this new house to help mold our family into one. There was a lot of work involved, and we all took part in making this new house a home. Barbara is known for her gift of interior design and is often asked for her opinion and help by other people who seek her advice for their own home decorating. She has the unique ability to go into an empty room and visualize how the room should look with the right kind of furniture, draperies and painting. When she is finished it not only matches, there is also an overwhelming heart-warming sense of peacefulness and relaxation that makes everyone feel comfortable and at home.

In addition to decorating and furnishing all the interior areas and flooring, we cleared about five acres of land around the house. We plowed two-acres; leveled, raked, and picked up every stone we could find, seeded it for our lawn and covered it with straw. (Being farm kids we knew how to do this.) In about three weeks we had one of the most beautiful lawns anyone had seen. With a new ranch-colonial house, mature maple trees in front of the house we had managed to protect during construction, it turned out to be a beautiful picturesque setting. We then picked out an ideal acre to cultivate our garden. As the brush piles grew and then shrank, our two families were becoming one.

Our new home soon became the hub for many church gatherings. We often invited the entire congregation for picnics, games, and fellowship with family, friends and visitors. Our large lawn was ready for outdoor potlucks and exciting volleyball games. There was a stream to wade in, woods for firewood and plenty of acreage for all to roam. We wanted our home to always bring forth the warm pervasive glow of caring hospitality, and Christian love. We also wanted it to be an oasis of security, joy, and spiritual insight.

About one and a half years later after bonding our two families into one, God's next move occurred. It would be as dramatic for our family as taking the children. I had a **revolutionary encounter** with God that became the spiritual foundation to equip Barbara and me in raising godly children in an increasingly godless society.

That is the rest of our story of how God took two ordinary people who have a heart of obedience and created an extraordinary and transforming experience that has changed the lives of not only two families but a countless number of people. A story of divine revelation, transformational life choices, miraculous guidance and provision that led me and Barbara and our family to move across the country, establish and participate in Christian Schools, found a Christian ministry, write and distribute many books, booklets and newsletters, build two very successful businesses, build a Christian Retreat Center and call Christians to a "Campaign to Save Christian America."

By every description our life is a living demonstration of God's grace and mercy to a family and a nation, and can also be your story. Our prayer is that you can personally relate and have faith arise as you read our story, because God wants and can use you in some special way also.

God's next move in our life after taking these six children began when I visited my brother Dr. Charles Fraley in June, 1971.

FOUR

A REVOLUTIONARY
ENCOUNTER WITH GOD

In June 1971, almost a year and a half after taking the six children into our home, we took a trip to southwestern Ohio to visit my mom (my dad was no longer living), Barbara's parents and my brother Charles. On Sunday we stopped to see Charles and his wife, Marlene.

During our conversation, Charles asked me if I had spent much time studying the book of Revelation. "No," I said, "Mostly because I don't fully understand the highly-charged symbolism and metaphors of the text." Charles then began to tell me about the revelation he had received from the Lord concerning the identity of the end-time "beast" prophesied in Revelation chapter thirteen. I ask that you do not let the word revelation overwhelm you about an end-times prophecy. Read his testimony and the rest of this book. Before I share how I was impacted by what Charles had learned, let me share the testimony of my brother, Dr. Charles D. Fraley and how this unique revelation came about. He writes:

> When I graduated from high school in 1950, the
> U.S. was fighting the Korean War. Believing I

would be drafted, I joined the Navy. This proved to be a time of great testing for me. I found I was one of a few committed Christians in that branch of the service. Nevertheless, the Lord gave me the inward strength to live by God's biblical standards.

In fact, it was while I was in the Navy that the Lord gave me a desire to know Him better. I had a lot of spare time while on ship duty and was able to spend most of those hours reading and studying the Word of God. My normal practice was to rise two hours before wakeup call to pray, study the Word and memorize Scripture. By the time my four-year tour of duty was over I had memorized over eight hundred verses, word perfect, and would review about 150 of them every day.

It was during my Navy service I was led to commit my life to "full-time" Christian service. One day as I was reading Hebrews 13:5, *"Let your conversation be without covetousness; and be content with such things as you have: for he hath said, I will never leave thee, nor forsake thee"* (KJV). I felt the presence of God rise up in my spirit and surround me in a powerful way. At that moment I committed my life into the Lord's hands for whatever service He wanted me to do.

After military service, I was supported by the GI Bill and felt led to enter a Bible College in Nyack, New York. It was there I met, Marlene, the girl I would later marry. I learned later Marlene had made a commitment to serve the Lord in Africa as a missionary nurse. One evening a few months after entering Bible College, I asked God specifically what He wanted me to do with my life. I still had no clear career directive. My prayer was quickly followed by a vision. According to the Bible it is not unscriptural for the Lord to direct Christians through a vision or dream (see Job 33:15). However, any vision must be tested to be sure it is of the Lord by examining its fruit to see if it fits all of the spiritual principles found in the Word of God.

My vision was without ambiguity. I saw a man standing over the ocean with one foot in Africa and the other in America. The man was dressed in doctor's clothing with doctor's gear and saying: "Come over and help, come over and help." I later learned that this call was similar to the Macedonian call Paul the Apostle experienced in Acts: 16:9. As I asked the Lord for the meaning of this vision, the Spirit of the Lord convicted me that I was to become a doctor and go to Africa to help the poor and needy.

I was stunned. This was a completely new thought to me. I had never thought about being a doctor, nor was I even familiar with what was involved in becoming a doctor. When I committed my life to the Lord I thought I would be a farmer. At the same time, I was just waiting for the Lord to show me what He wanted me to do.

After one year of Bible school I took a step of faith and transferred to pre-med at Taylor University a Christian liberal arts university, in Upland,

Indiana. After completing my pre-med work at Taylor, I went to medical school at Ohio State University. After my graduation, I served one year of internship and four years of surgical residency at Saint Elisabeth Hospital in Youngstown, Ohio. After passing the National Exams of the American Board of Surgery, I became a fully Board-Certified General Surgeon.

However, during my thirteen years of preparation, I had somehow slipped in my spiritual walk with the Lord and my vision to be a medical missionary in Africa dimmed. I rationalized I could practice medicine and serve the Lord just as well in the states. This would enable me, my wife Marlene and our two children, to enjoy all the benefits available to doctors in the U.S. Besides, I thought, if I ever did go to Africa it would be good to have some practical experience. Several doctor friends and other Christians agreed with me.

The truth is that without realizing it I had gradually fallen into **deception**. How it happened is actually hard for me to say. It seemed to develop in subtle ways over time. I justified it with the idea that even though I was going to practice medicine in the U.S., I would still be willing at some point to go to Africa.

I began my medical practice in the area where I grew up. Year by year my practice increased. I was soon earning a yearly net income of $300,000.00 to $400,000.00. That was in the early 1970s. I had my own airplane and the nicest Buick one could buy and our family had a comfortable home in town. I bought the 100-acre family farm where most of my brothers and sisters had grown up. I outfitted it with tractors, a pickup truck, animals and horses. I was able to buy and pay cash for about everything anyone in our family wanted.

While my medical practice flourished, however, something was wrong spiritually. I was walking in direct disobedience to the Lord's original call for my life, namely, to serve the Lord cross-culturally. I had fallen prey to the influence and lure of secular humanism.

The worst was yet to come. It happened about four years into my medical practice when I got involved in an unscriptural situation. Believing one should be careful to write only what is helpful for the building up, and in consideration of others, I choose not to share the details of that situation, other than to say it had the potential of destroying everything I had, including my family. That, of course, is what the deceiver Satan wanted. As in all of life's experiences, good and bad, there are important lessons to be learned. Although God is merciful and long suffering, He calls us to live our lives according to biblical principles. When God says we are to come out of the world and be separate, He really means just that (See 2 Corinthians 6:16-18).

As a physician of many years, I often have to deal with, and attempt to assist Christians, including pastors and church leaders, with problems they would rather not share with other people. Any of

the sins listed in Galatians 5:19 as the "desires of
our sinful nature" can make us insensitive and dull
our receptivity to God's Holy Spirit in our lives. I
had been **deceived** by the enemy and fell prey to
the many attractions and lures of the world. This
in turn, brought about disobedience to the Lord
and a major spiritual defeat in my life.

I was delivered from this **deception** by a
Christian who challenged me about my lifestyle.
Through questioning, the Spirit convicted me and
opened my spiritual eyes to see the condition of
my disobedient heart. **I was devastated**. From my
youth I had had such a strong desire to serve the
Lord. I could not believe I had strayed so from the
Lord's will. The irony is that during this time I
was still active in church. I was studying the Scriptures and spending time in prayer.

After the veil of **deception** had been lifted,
I began to seek the Lord with a true heart of
repentance. I asked the Lord for a new filling of
the Holy Spirit and the power to walk with him
according to his will. <u>For the next seven months
I put forth every ounce of my being into seeking
God, studying the Word, meditating, praying and
worshiping Him in a state of repentance.</u> I also
wanted to know <u>why so many Christians seemed
to be living such defeated lives.</u>

At the end of the seven months, my family
and I went on a two-week vacation to Florida.
I had decided to spend this time fasting, praying and seeking the Lord, still in a spirit of

repentance. I was determined not to stop until I knew beyond a shadow of a doubt that I was filled with the Holy Spirit.

Midway through the second week of our vacation, I awakened one night and knew the presence of the Lord was in the room with me in a special way. I then began to have visions similar to the one where the Lord had called me to become a doctor and go to Africa. It should be noted that these visions only came when I was living in complete victory and holiness.

The first vision was that of a large head of a beast—very fat looking—hovering over America and swallowing up Christians. The Spirit of the Lord showed me the meaning of this vision. This beast represented the power of materialism and pleasure in our country. It was swallowing up many Christians by spiritually **deceiving** and overcoming them through the influence of the materialism and pleasure. This is what had first pulled me away and caused my disobedience in not going to the mission field.

The Lord did not give me the full identity of the "beast" I saw in my vision. However, He did convict me that I had been caught up in this beast's system and had been overcome by it. I was convicted this "beast," working through the powerful temptations of materialism and pleasure, was causing Christians in America to lose their spiritual power. This is why I believe so many have become apathetic toward the deterioration of the biblical standards in our country. It is also why so many Christians in America are experiencing major spiritual defeats as thousands of families are being ruptured through divorce and their children falling under the influence of our secular society.

The enemy is using the system of this "beast" as a powerful tool to attack and destroy America's biblically based moral standards. These are Christian principles that have guided the majority of Americans since the founding of our country. Never before has our spiritual enemy, Satan, been able to attack and change the standards of a society in such a short time as he has in America during this last generation.

I am not saying the Lord showed me it's wrong to have material things or enjoy good wholesome pleasure. What the Spirit of the Lord did reveal to me through the vision of this "beast" is how the desire for material things in our country, and the exposure to immoral practices through the entertainment industry, have become so strong it is causing Christians to fall prey to **deception**.

The Bible teaches that DECEPTION BREEDS COMPROMISE! Compromise is disobedience to the standards of God's Word, which brings about spiritual defeat. That is how Satan used **deception** to get Eve, then Adam, to sin in the Garden of Eden. I saw that Satan is continually bombarding our minds, with ungodly and unscriptural ideas and principles using television, radio and the media as false teachers.

Following the first vision I quickly had four other visions of Jesus Christ. Scriptures tell us the Holy Spirit always testifies of Jesus.

The first vision I had of Jesus showed Him giving up His life, willing to pay the ultimate price on the cross, for the salvation of mankind. The next vision showed Jesus was a disciplined person, one whom had His face set as a flint to fulfill the purpose of His incarnation. The third vision of Jesus showed me the great love Jesus has for mankind. The last vision of Jesus showed Him standing at the door of my heart knocking wanting to come in and re-establish His will in my life.

When I awoke the next morning, I still sensed the presence of the Lord and I was drawn to read the passage in Revelation that dealt specifically with the prophecy of the beast. When I came to Revelation chapter thirteen, the Spirit of the Lord seemed to literally take verse 3 off the page and sear its full meaning into my mind. Revelation 13:3 reads: *"One of the heads of the beast seemed to have had a fatal wound, but the fatal wound had been healed. The whole world was astonished and followed the beast."*

In an instant, I had a perfect understanding of the exact event that fulfilled the wound of the beast in this verse. It was as if I had known it all my life. What the Lord seared into my mind was the fulfillment of this prophecy, written nearly 2000 years ago by the Apostle John. Namely, this "wound of the beast," was the event of the surprise attack by the Japanese on Pearl Harbor, December 7, 1941.

The attack at Pearl Harbor devastated America's Pacific Naval Fleet and all of our nation's Air Force installations in Hawaii.

At first I had several problems with this revelation. My first reaction was, "that is impossible." My problem was because from my previous Bible studies, the most common interpretation was that the events mentioned in the book were to take place sometime in the future. That is, from the 4th chapter on. However, if this revelation was true, the events prophesied in the book of Revelation were already taking place and some of it was already history, including this particular verse.

Another shock was, if the "wound of the beast" was the attack on Pearl Harbor that meant this "beast" in Revelation thirteen was the United States government, which has become the greatest superpower in the history of mankind. That was hard for me to accept. I had always been taught it would be a particular man who would rise up and rule the world and somehow be associated with the European Economic Community. I never associated the United States as being a major part of this development. The thought never occurred to me that the prophet Daniel was told the word "beast" meant "empires" or what we today call "superpowers." The Apostle John was being consistent by using the word "beast" in the same way in his prophecy about the major superpower in the last days.

My brother Bob and I want to make clear that identifying the United States government as the "beast" superpower of Revelation thirteen, we are not suggesting that Americans should not love their country, pray for our government leaders, honor the flag, and be thankful for living in a free country. Quite the contrary! Our desire is to preserve Christian standards in our country along with our great spiritual history and to equip Christians for these last days. We believe our enemy, Satan, is on the attack to destroy "Christian America."

For several days I resisted this revelation from the Lord. But the Lord would not give me peace until I fully accepted the fact that this prophecy about the "wound of the beast" was fulfilled at Pearl Harbor. When I finally gave in, the Lord anointed me with an overpowering anointing of His Holy Spirit. I seemed to literally vibrate with spiritual power. All I could do was lift up my hands, as if I could actually touch the Lord, and praise the Holy name of Jesus over and over. This special immersion in the power of the Holy Spirit lasted for about six weeks. It served as a confirmation from the Lord that the revelation I had received about the "wound of the beast" and the identification of the "beast" in Revelation thirteen was truth.

During the time the Lord's special anointing was resting on me, I constantly witnessed for the Lord Jesus Christ seemingly without effort. And though my words were often no different than at other times, when I had witnessed, my words just flowed out and there was an unbelievable difference in the effect on people who heard me. Whether I spoke one on one or at a church, nearly everyone who listened would come under a heavy conviction of repentance, recommitment, and some had a born again experience with the Lord. Of course, none of this had anything to do with me. It was all the power of the Holy Spirit.

About two weeks after this anointing, or baptism as some would call it, as I was literally immersed in the power of the Holy Spirit—just as real as if I was immersed in water—my younger brother, Bob, came by for a visit. I was so filled with this revelation I couldn't help but share these things with him. I had no thought of trying to convince him that they were true. I just shared what actually happened to me. I had no idea it would affect him one way or the other. Bob later shared with me that the anointing of the Holy Spirit came upon him in a powerful and similar way as it had to me. The Spirit of the Lord convicted him that what I was sharing about the "beast" was true, and the bondage of being attached to the things of this world was suddenly broken and the presence of the Lord Jesus became so real to him and has existed ever since. Bob shares that this anointing fills his every day in such a way his focus is completely on serving the Lord Jesus Christ and fulfilling His will and purpose in his life.

Interestingly, God has inspired Bob to do a tremendous amount of study and research, literally thousands of hours to see whether Scripture could support such a revelation. All that I saw in the Spirit at that time has now been confirmed as being in harmony with God's revealed Word. The Bible also states that in the mouth of two witnesses shall a thing be established. Here was another confirmation that this was of the Lord.

After about six weeks when I had this special anointing, the Lord seemed to lift His special anointing. I then came under a period of heavy testing by the enemy. I do not say much about what happened during this time of testing because it was too awful and too scary for me to even talk about. The one comment I will make about this experience is that I know for certain there is a being called Satan, and a place called Hell. It seemed they unleashed all their powers upon me. However, I did learn that: *"Greater is He that is in us, than he that is in the world"* (see 1 John 4:4), and that by trusting in God's Word, we can stand against him (Satan).

Since that time, I have walked with a certain "holy fear" that has helped me to stay in the Lord's will and follow His commandments. It actually resulted in me and my wife making the necessary preparations to go to the mission field in Africa. We first went to Tanzania, East Africa for a year and afterwards to Kenya where we served the Lord for 29 years.

An important truth we learn from Scripture is Satan attacks, at times fiercely, anything God has raised up for His glory. As you study America's spiritual development God often intervened and that is why we became a Christian nation and the center of Christianity in these last days. Therefore, we should expect that our country would be in for some heavy spiritual warfare in these last days. Revelation chapter thirteen is referred to as the end-time spiritual warfare chapter. It is understandable why America plays a major role in this prophecy. Bob discusses all of this and much more very clearly in his recent book, *You Are Salt & Light: Equipping Christians for These Last Days.* Check his web site www.bobfraleychristianlifeoutreach.com.

I close my testimony by sharing a short summary of my ministry in Kenya that came after this remarkable revelation. It was written by someone in Kenya who said:

"Dr. Charles Fraley, M.D., and his wife, Marlene, R.N., began serving the Lord on the mission field in Africa in 1974. Dr. Fraley became the Medical Coordinator and Executive Director of a large health ministry in Kenya with a list of responsibilities that seems endless. He shared the love of Christ as he oversaw five hospitals and over fifty health centers and dispensaries throughout the entire country.

"Dr. Fraley delivered supplies, checked on patients, performed surgery, as well as assisted in administration, teaching of the staff and encouraging each facility. His duties required him to spend many days away from home traveling over dirt, rock, and sand roads and foot paths. He also faced risk traveling

among the African tribes and wild animals, which
at times posed life-threatening danger. In addition,
when he traveled out into the bush country, he lived
as the natives—eating their food, and sometimes
sleeping in his vehicle or under the stars.

"From 1976-1980, Dr. Fraley and his wife were
involved in building a new hospital and establish-
ing a school of nursing on one of the largest mission
stations of its kind in the world at Kijabe, Kenya.
The hospital provides one of the highest qualities
of health care of any mission hospital, not only in
Kenya but throughout East Africa. The quality of
training Dr. Fraley and his staff developed at the
nursing school is as good as any in western civiliza-
tion. All staff members in this health ministry must
profess Jesus as Lord and Savior and maintain high
Christian standards.

"Dr. and Mrs. Fraley also assisted and worked
with the Kenyan government in obtaining licenses
for many of the long and short-term missionary
doctors and nurses coming into the country. He par-
ticipated with missionaries from different mission
organizations in Bible study and prayer groups for
their spiritual growth. He was the attending physician for many of the missionaries of all denominations that come into the country. For over ten years
sat on the Board of Mission for Essential Drugs,
an organization he helped establish in order to get
medicines at cost for Mission Health Services. He
also served as Board Member and Vice Treasurer of
the Christian Health Association of Kenya (CHAK).

This organization was developed to serve all of the Protestant Health Services in Kenya consisting of over 260 health units.

"The President of Kenya asked that Dr. Fraley take over a major health center among the poor people in a remote area of the country. He agreed to do this, not only to meet the desperate health needs of these people, but to provide a great opportunity to share the love and salvation of our Lord Jesus Christ. All of the fifty-seven health units under his development and direction minister to the poor and needy in remote areas. Other projects included his involvement in the building of a crippled children's hospital and the building of a medical training facility and expansion of the nurses training center.

"This barely touches the surface of all that has happened for the Lord through the ministry of Dr. Fraley and his wife, as well as others with whom they worked. God blessed them to lead a team of godly and committed Christians to develop these many ministries. All of the glory, praise, and honor, must go to the Lord. As you can see, there was more work to be done than there were hours in a day. Only the power and anointing of the Holy Spirit could give a man the strength to accomplish all that Dr. Charles Fraley accomplished during his thirty years of ministry in Africa.

"Dr. Fraley and his wife are among those godly servants who forsook their material possessions, family ties, pleasures, home and country to follow the call of our Lord Jesus—to serve wherever He leads to help the poor and needy of the world. They are not seen

on TV nor do you hear much about them, as they are not in the public eye. They labored selflessly, day in and day out, to share the love and salvation of our Lord Jesus Christ, and reach out to the needs of the sick, hurting, and needy people of this world. Their ministry was built on solid rock. They stood the test of time in their obedience and faithfulness."

At age of seventy and working under the auspices of African Inland Missions, my brother Dr. Charles Fraley was required to retire. As of this writing, he and his wife moved to Florida where they continue to help the many ministries in Kenya that he founded and directed by occasionally traveling to Kenya plus raising support here in the States to help the poor and needy. (See Appendix A for more information and my web site.)

If you ask Dr. Fraley or me, we both respond in a similar way. Our lives were totally transformed in our relationship with the Lord following the remarkable revelation we received that identified the "beast-superpower" in Revelation chapter thirteen.

The special anointing from the Lord not only broke the bondage to the things of this world, but also placed a gift of "holy fear" within our souls that has driven our commitment of obedience to the Lord since that day. Our sensing the presence of the Lord Jesus has been constant and biblical truths seem to leap off the pages as our faith soared. The best way to confirm our anointing is to look at the fruit in our lives since that day of our revolutionary encounter with the Lord in 1971.

My brother and I continue to marvel at the faithfulness of God in our lives. We are intrigued with the fact that even though we both had a similar revolutionary experience, the Lord, after this revelation, sent us in completely different directions.

We were both directed to give up everything. For my brother and his wife it was a successful medical practice and all of their possessions. For me and my wife it was my position as a corporate executive, my company Cadillac and the beautiful new dream home my wife and I built on our fifteen acres. Then, in obedience to the Lord's leading and without my having any job prospects to support our family, we traveled 2,250 miles across the country with a caravan of vehicles and our family to a totally new territory. My brother was directed to go to Africa as a missionary doctor, the field in which he was trained. Later I was directed to re-enter the business world, the field for which I had been trained, and then use my resources to help support the body of Christ. It was this revelation that became the foundation and cornerstone that equipped Barbara and me in building our spiritual ark for the saving of our family in these troubled times, which you will be reading more about.

One of the lessons to be learned from how the Lord directed each of our lives after receiving this revelation is how the Lord blesses and honors a heart of obedience when we seek and are committed to carrying out His will for our lives, regardless of what that may be.

The major event prophesied about in these last days that identifies the "wound of the beast" was the bombing of Pearl Harbor. Before continuing Barbara's and my testimony I will give you a glimpse of my research into this event. Over the years, as I have shared this revelation, this has been of great interest to people.

FIVE

THE EVENT THAT CHANGED AMERICA FOREVER

For some, Christmas can be a painful time. But when I was growing up, the month of December was the most magical month of all. When I was seven, I recall going to bed on a Saturday evening when there were only nineteen days before that wondrous morning, and thinking what I wanted more than anything else under the tree was a new pair of shoes.

This may sound strange to people who grew up in an age of progressive prosperity where Christmas was celebrated with the giving and receiving of extra gifts of toys and clothing. But this was on the edge of the Great Depression, an event unprecedented in American history. It was an event that made an indelible impression on my parents' generation and left millions with invisible scars that for many never healed.

At its lowest point during the decade of the 1930s, a staggering 25% of the country's labor-force was without work. In our nation's cities, thousands of people built makeshift shelters in empty lots, and garbage dumps were regularly scavenged by the hungry in search of food. But this economic stagflation was soon to end when on September 3, 1939, Great Britain (with its commonwealth countries) and France declared war on Nazi Germany for its invasion of Poland. In the spring of 1940, German forces suddenly overran Denmark and Norway, then Holland, Luxembourg, Belgium and Northern France. Hitler's war machine scattered the French army and forced 150,000 men of the British Expeditionary Force to a jam-packed channel beach at Dunkirk.

President Roosevelt, in office for a third term, had expressed misgivings about once again committing American soldiers to fight on European soil. However, in the interest of National Defense, he urged Congress to be pro-active and ratchet up production of war materials. This included a yearly production of 50,000 airplanes and the manufacturing of war supplies for purchase by countries threatened by the Axis powers of Germany and Italy. This massive demand for the implements of war soon put thousands of unemployed Americans back to work, which officially ended the era of the Great Depression.

Even an impartial observer would have said the outlook in Europe was bleak. Equally unsettling news was coming out of the Far East. Japan, already at war with China, joined the Axis in 1940 and was aggressively moving on many fronts. So all in all it was a nervous time. Nevertheless, the truth was that most Americans saw these battles as far away, and they wanted to keep things that way. We were a humble, peace-loving, Christian nation that deplored war and was extremely reluctant to get involved once more in its killing fields.

All of this, of course, went totally by me. I was too young to pay attention. The morning of December 7, 1941 however, changed my world and that of all Americans in a most profound way. On that day, millions across the States huddled around their radios to hear the news. Confusion, disbelief and shock spread across the land. America had been attacked for the first time in more than a century. The Japanese had bombed Pearl Harbor. An unthinkable event had taken place ... a day that would change America, forever.

In the spring of 1940, a large segment of the U.S. Pacific Fleet was stationed at Pearl Harbor. It was the world's greatest aggregation of warships—a million tons of fighting steel. But the U.S. influence in the Pacific irritated the Japanese. While Hitler had conquered most of Western Europe, the island empire of Japan saw a golden opportunity to expand into Southeast Asia. But Japan feared our significant naval presence in the Pacific threatened their ambitious plans. In December 1940, Fleet Admiral Isoroku Yamamoto, Commander in Chief of Japan's Combined Fleet, convinced the Japanese Imperial Council to consider using their aircraft carriers to launch a surprise attack against the Pacific Fleet at Pearl Harbor. He reasoned for Japan to achieve supremacy on the high seas, it had to neutralize America's military capacity.

Yamamoto's plan was to literally catch the U.S. sleeping. He knew that just as a weaker judo expert can throw a stronger opponent by catching him off balance, Japan needed to seize the initiative. By striking a fatal blow in one daring attack, they would gain a strategic military edge in the Pacific. He and his advisors concluded that if Japan gained such an advantage for twelve months, they could win the war in the Pacific against the United States.

Yamamoto's idea had merit. As late as February 19, 1941 Pennsylvania Congressman Charles I. Faddis reflected the perspective of the majority in the United States when he said:

> *The Japanese are not going to risk a fight with a first-class nation. They are unprepared to do so, and no one knows that better than they do. They will not*

> *dare to get into a position where they must face the*
> *American Navy in open battle. Their Navy is not*
> *strong enough and their homeland is too vulnerable.*

It took a year of intense preparations for the Japanese to ready themselves for war against the U.S. This planning had to be done in the strictest secrecy. If the strike did not catch the United States napping, the plan would fail.

The Japanese strategic military planners had several problems to solve before they could launch their first strike mission. They had to design and build special torpedoes capable of operating in Pearl Harbor's shallow waters. They had to produce new armor-piercing shells deliverable from planes flying from low altitudes. And they had to select and train pilots how to fly in low attack formation. They also had to organize a naval task force and teach the personnel how to refuel the ships in the rough seas of the northern Pacific Ocean, the route selected to avoid detection and assure complete surprise. Prior to our Manhattan Project (the development of the atomic bomb), the Japanese Pearl Harbor plan was the most highly classified, closely guarded and best-kept secret of World War II.

At 6 o'clock on the morning of November 26, 1941, the Japanese strike force weighed anchor. Eleven days later, just before dawn on December 7, they reached the launching point for their raid, 230 miles due north of the island of Oahu, Hawaii. Their task force of 33 warships, including six aircraft carriers, had successfully sailed a northern route through rough waters and dense fog to avoid detection by American ships and surveillance aircraft.

The attack that Sunday morning came with startling swiftness. On every Japanese carrier, the scene was the same. Airplane engines sputtered to life, signal flags fluttered up and down, as one by one the aircraft roared down the flight decks, drowning out the cheers and yells from the crews. Plane after plane rose in the sky, flashing in the early morning sun that peeked over the horizon. This airborne armada consisted of 353 planes. At the time it was the largest concentration of airpower in the history of warfare. On the peaceful target island, American sailors were totally unaware of the tremendous fighting force that would soon send many of them to a watery grave. Perfect timing was essential. Our enemy knew full well if anything went wrong, the attack could fail. But they were dead on course. Their mission was the destruction of the Pacific Fleet stationed at Pearl Harbor and all of the nearby U.S. Air Force installations.

It was 7:40 a.m. when the first Japanese pilots sighted Oahu's coastline. Mitsuo Fuchida, the commander who led the first formation of planes (he became a Christian after the war), later wrote: "The harbor was still asleep in the morning mist." The element of surprise remained with the Japanese. As the first wave of planes approached Pearl Harbor, they deployed into three groups. They first struck and destroyed the air bases to prevent U.S. fighter planes from counterattacking. They hit Hickam Air Force Base, Wheeler Field, Bellows Field, Kaneohe Naval Base and the Naval Air Station at Ford Island.

The Japanese pilots flew in at treetop level, bringing with them massive destruction. Hangars were burned, barracks were razed, and hundreds of men were killed that fateful morning. A total of 341 U.S. planes were destroyed while still on the ground. Since the air bases were so close together, the attacks all came at the same time. Everything happened at once. But the assault on the airfields was only the beginning of this awful drama. In the harbor were 96 warships of the United States Pacific Fleet. Included were eight cruisers, 29 destroyers, five submarines, assorted mine craft and eight U.S. battleships: the West Virginia, Arizona, Oklahoma, Nevada, Tennessee, Pennsylvania, California and Maryland.

USS Arizona before bombing[1]

At approximately 8:10 a.m., the battleship USS Arizona was hit by a 1760-pound armor-piercing bomb that slammed through her deck and ignited the main fuel tank and exploded. The force of the explosion was so great it raised the bow of the ship completely out of the water and split her right behind the number one gun turret. The Arizona sank in less than nine minutes. Of her crew of 1543 men, 1177 lost their lives.

Struck by several torpedoes, the USS Oklahoma completely rolled over, trapping some 400 men inside. The California and West Virginia sank at their moorings, while the Utah, which had

USS Arizona after bombing[1]

been converted to a training ship, capsized with a loss of more than fifty of her crew. The Maryland, Pennsylvania and Tennessee all suffered significant damage. The Nevada attempted to run out to sea but took several hits and had to be beached to avoid sinking and blocking the harbor entrance.

As the Japanese dive-bombers rocked the harbor, the mammoth gray ships along Battleship Row, writhing from the explosions of bombs and torpedoes, burned at their moorings, sending billows of black smoke into the morning sky. The invaders dealt crippling blows to ship after ship. Most of the damage was done in the first fifteen minutes.

The attack on Pearl Harbor ended at about 9:45 a.m. In less than two hours the Japanese had immobilized most of the U.S. air strength and nearly eliminated their chief objective, the U.S. Pacific Fleet. A once mighty military fortress had been pulverized. As the drone of enemy formations disappeared over the horizon, heading back to their carriers, they left behind a scene of horrible chaos, crackling flames, hissing steam and dying men. Half-submerged ships were strewn about the harbor, tilting at crazy angles. Wreckage floated across the oily surface of the water as human bodies began to wash ashore.

As the smoke began to clear, U.S. forces began to assess the damage. Twenty-two ships, including eight battleships, were sunk or heavily damaged, and more than 340 American aircraft had been destroyed. Japanese losses totaled 29 aircraft destroyed and 74 damaged. Before the war had begun, America had suffered one of the greatest defeats any nation ever endured. In addition, the Japanese had, in a couple of hours, seemingly secured mastery of the Far East.

Before the age of jet aircraft and nuclear weapons, battleships represented the ultimate in technological achievement and were the mightiest weapons of war. When a great ship sank like the Lusitanian, the Bismarck, or the Titanic, people listened to the details in amazement. Such occasions inspired legends, ballads and movies. Sinking ships were cataclysmic events akin to natural disasters like earthquakes and hurricanes.

Earlier, on the afternoon of the attack, First Lady Eleanor Roosevelt had talked to the nation by radio:

> *For months now, the knowledge that something of*
> *this kind might happen has been hanging over our*
> *heads.... We now know what we have to face, and we*
> *know we are ready to face it. Whatever is ahead of us,*
> *I am sure we can accomplish it; we are the free and*
> *unconquerable people of the United States of America.*

The next day, President Roosevelt asked Congress to declare war on Japan. His request carried almost unanimously. His famous words to the American public: "Yesterday, December 7, 1941—a day which will live in infamy—the United States of America was suddenly and deliberately attacked by naval and air forces of the Empire of Japan."

Historians refer to this attack as one of the great turning points in world history. At the time, Hitler viewed this defeat as a mortal wound to our military strength, and declared war on the United States on December 11. The Japanese General Tojo was convinced that for all practical purposes, the war was over. But he never could have been more wrong. Instead, the attack on Pearl Harbor galvanized the United States into astonishing activity. Here was a catalytic moment that eventually would spell defeat for the Axis.

Winston Churchill wrote:

> *Hitler's fate was sealed. Mussolini's fate was sealed. As for the Japanese, they would be ground to powder.... United we could subdue everybody else in the world. Many disasters, immeasurable cost and tribulation lay ahead, but there was no more doubt about the end.*

Almost immediately, men from every state formed long lines at draft boards, clamoring to join in the service of their country. As U.S. soldiers marched off to war, victory gardens sprang up, recycling bins appeared, and gas-rationing cards were introduced. Factories that produced autos were converted into making jeeps, tanks and airplanes. The attack that was supposed to be fatal actually energized the fighting spirit of Americans as little else could have done. The United States jumped to its feet to become a fearsome warrior. During the next three and a half years, we forged a war machine that helped conquer enemy forces on two different fronts, in Europe and Asia. America was transformed from a provincial, regional power to a technological, military and political titan stretching across both hemispheres, forever changing the American way of life.

To understand what happened at Pearl Harbor, and what led up to it, the book *At Dawn We Slept* by Gordon W. Prange is considered by many to be the final word. His work has been praised as "definitive," "a masterpiece," "authoritative," "unparalleled" and "impossible to forget." Prange was uniquely qualified for writing this book. He was educated at the University of Iowa and the University of Berlin. Later, he taught history at the University of Maryland. From October 1946 to June 1951, Prange was chief of General Douglas MacArthur's G-2 Historical Section located at General HQ, Far East Command, Tokyo.

From his training and firsthand knowledge, Prange knew more about the attack on Pearl Harbor than any other person. He also interviewed virtually every surviving Japanese officer who took part in the Pearl Harbor operation, as well as all pertinent sources on the U.S. side. His 873-page history of the attack is based on thirty-seven years of research. His work is acclaimed worldwide and is an invaluable reference. It was used as a major source in making the movie, Tora! Tora! Tora!

He writes:

> *The Japanese gave each American a personal stake in*
> *the titanic struggle for the minds and bodies of mankind*
> *[that] raged in Europe and Asia. After December 7, 1941,*
> *Americans no longer could look upon the war from*
> *a distance as an impersonal, ideological conflict. The*
> *sense of outrage triggered a feeling of direct involve-*
> *ment [that] resulted in an explosion of national*

energy. The Japanese gave the average American a
cause he could understand and believe to be worth
fighting for. Thus, in a very special way Pearl Harbor
became the turning point of the world struggle.

On December 7, 1991 George Bush, our 41st President, jour-
neyed to Hawaii to revisit Pearl Harbor on the 50th anniversary
of the attack. The years have since slipped by quickly, and new
generations of Americans have all but forgotten the tragedy of that
infamous Sunday morning. However, for any who visit that site, it
remains a grim reminder of a defeat that propelled our country into
the fierce vortex of sacrifice, suffering and war. What happened
that day will live forever through the Arizona Memorial, dedicated
on Memorial Day, 1962.

USS Arizona Memorial[1]

The memorial was designed with a sag in the middle. Solid white walls and a roof compose two ends of the rectangular building, exposing a thin archway of bare, white ribs. The depressed center was purposely designed to express the initial wound to a great nation, and the sturdy ends to express its earlier strength and eventual recovery and victory.

Today, the *USS Arizona* rests peacefully in an upright position under 38 feet of water at the bottom of Pearl Harbor. Visitors stand atop the wreckage inside the Arizona Memorial to look down at the remains of the sunken ship. Oil still rises from her rusting hull, and the 1100 men still entombed there provide a silent but eloquent witness to the horror of defeat.

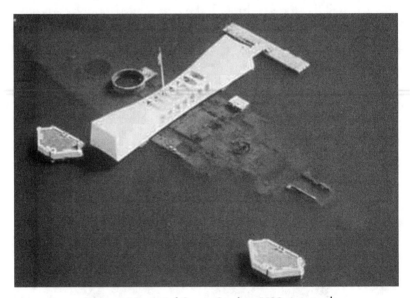

Arizona Memorial Spans Sunken USS Arizona[1]

The attack was so sudden, so spectacular and so devastating; Congress convened a joint committee to investigate. The committee's findings filled 40 volumes. This single attack set into motion forces that changed forever the way Americans work, play, build families and conduct their lives. Our involvement in the war transformed our land from a provincial isolationist country to a superpower—a technological hothouse of incredible economic political and military power.

There can be little doubt but that this was a defining event that forever changed who we are as a people. It's not like an earlier version of 9/11/01. It's far and beyond the scope of that day, as awful as that day was. It was Pearl Harbor that put the United States on a path that would lead almost inevitably to us becoming the world's great superpower in these last days!

On December 7, 2011, it will be seven decades since that "day which will live in infamy." It's understandable if these recollections seem far removed from today's headlines. Time passes quickly, and it seems even important leaders are here today and gone tomorrow. It would also be a daunting task to put together a definitive list of important changes in our world over the past seventy years. The United States is a vastly different nation than it was in 1941 on that day that changed America. One of those differences is that while we as a nation have become prosperous, powerful and proud, many have become profane. Profane means to treat the sacred with an attitude of contempt. Many dismiss Christianity as more or less irrelevant for moderns. For some it goes beyond ignoring the church to ridiculing and debasing it. It's almost as if there is an unstated national effort to distance ourselves from our Christian past. There is a new emphasis on tolerance that demands "Christian America" be thought of as a term that's outdated, embarrassing and even offensive.

---

1. Photographs of the USS Arizona and the USS Arizona Memorial are assumed to be in the public domain. These images were reproduced for educational purposes. An unsuccessful attempt was made by the author to discover the identity of the photographers in order to credit them for their work.

SIX

MY NOAH EXPERIENCE

When my brother Charles shared his revelation that identified the "beast/superpower" of Revelation chapter 13, the Lord did something in my life that I had never before experienced. There is no way to really describe such an experience except that suddenly I could not help but tremble as the power of God fell on me. The power was overwhelming and I experienced an inner presence of Jesus that filled my heart. He became so real I nearly fell to my knees. I knew immediately, without a doubt, what my brother was telling me about the identity of this "beast" in Revelation chapter 13 was true.

I called this revolutionary encounter I had with the Lord in 1971 my Noah experience. I say that because Hebrews 11:7 says, *"By faith Noah, when warned about things not yet seen, in holy fear built an ark to save his family."* The Lord used the identity of this "beast/superpower" to warn Barbara and me about the tremendous spiritual warfare the enemy would be waging against Christian values in America.

Believing God's revelation about things not seen, placed a "holy fear" in both of us. And like Noah, we began to build an ark to save our family. This wasn't a physical ark of course, but a spiritual ark that was to protect our family against the heavy spiritual warfare that was to come in America. Looking back nearly 40 years later, we can see it has happened as the rapid deterioration of our country's moral values has devastated many Christian families. This revelation from the Lord became our spiritual foundation for the saving of our family. You will learn as you continue to read how this has been carried out over the last forty years. As we walked by faith before the Lord with a "holy fear," this equipped us with a heart of obedience to be used for His service in these last days.

Before I continue, let me make a comment about how this word "beast" is used in prophecy. When the word "beast" is used in prophetic Scripture, many Christians believe it refers to some ugly, foul, evil monstrosity. However, that is not how Scripture depicts the use of this word. We are fortunate the prophet Daniel had a vision of "beasts" and sought its meaning from God. An angel told Daniel the word "beast" referred to what in his day was called an empire or kingdom, and what today we now call a superpower.

There is no better authority in understanding the meaning of something in Scripture than to compare Scripture with Scripture. Therefore, if Daniel was told the word "beast" meant superpower, that tells us that in the Book of Revelation chapter 13, John would also most likely be speaking about a superpower in these last days.

I don't know where you may be in your understanding of the times in which we are living, but most Christians, including many Bible scholars and our country's spiritual leaders, believe we are living in the last days or end-times. They base their reasoning on the many prophetic Scriptures that have been fulfilled.

However, don't be overwhelmed by what the Lord revealed to my brother Charles and then to me that identified this "beast" or "superpower" in these last days. From everything we have learned from Scripture, it makes perfect sense. I believe America, has had a special calling from God. Other than the nation of Israel, I could not find where God ever came close to intervening in the spiritual development of a nation's history to the extent He has in America.

I reference the historical events of the Pilgrims, the Puritans, the Great Awakening, our Constitution being based on biblical principles, the many other great revivals throughout our history, and the establishment of thousands of Christian churches throughout our land and more. Think of all the missionary ministries the people of America have sponsored to help needy people throughout the world. I believe we have become the center of Christianity in these last days.

One of the first things the Lord began to teach me after this revelation that identified this "beast/superpower" in Revelation 13 was how important it was to understand the tactics and methods of our spiritual enemy Satan. Most Christians I've discovered know very little about our spiritual enemy. I was intrigued by this when I realized that in every human endeavor, be it military, sports, business or whatever, we are taught to know our competition or our enemy. This is important in order to properly prepare a defense against our enemy's offense. We seem to follow this practice for everything except the most important of all, which is to understand the tactics of our spiritual enemy. Many Christians therefore are unprepared and have very little understanding about the tactics and methods of our spiritual enemy, Satan.

In my book, *You are Salt & Light: Equipping Christians For These Last Days,* I remind people that Satan has always tried to sabotage the work of God's people and His kingdom. This is why in these last days, Satan is on the attack in America by dragging down Christian leaders, destroying Christian homes, mocking Christian values, and attacking the foundations of our nation.

Also, as John prophesies in Revelation 13, Satan (called "dragon") will attack us by working through our worldly superpower position, prophetically called a "beast," by attempting to destroy "Christian America." From everything we learn from Scripture about our enemy we should expect this to happen.

Let me give you a true life example that illustrates this principle. An elderly gentleman I knew decided to start a new manufacturing business in Miami, Florida. He was successful in his business and owned manufacturing plants in the north—Ohio, St. Louis, Minneapolis and Baltimore. There were already four other manufacturing plants similar to his in Miami and when their owners became aware of my friend's plans to open a new plant in Miami, they offered him a million dollars not to build a plant in Miami. They knew he would be a tough competitor and did not want him there.

My friend reasoned that if his competitors were willing to pay him a million dollars to get rid of him, then Miami must be a good lucrative business area for the product he made. Therefore, he decided he would definitely proceed to build the plant.

Using the same logic, and knowing that God has used and is using America in unique ways for the extension of His Kingdom, Satan has declared spiritual war on America and wants to destroy our country's Christian heritage and influence. America has been the strongest spiritual bulwark against the wicked influences of Satan. His efforts to destroy America's influence as the center of Christianity confirms God's special calling for America in these last days and why Satan has launched a spiritual attack to weaken and destroy if possible our Christian values. That is what John is prophesying about in Revelation 13, which is often called the end-times spiritual warfare chapter.

It was so important to God that we understand that our spiritual enemy would conduct this spiritual warfare through this "beast/superpower," that He gave us Revelation 13 to describe its identity in detail. There are several unique descriptive verses in this chapter that describe the characteristics of this "beast/superpower."

Through my research and study I found our country fits every one of these unique descriptive characteristics. Not one other nation even comes close. I explain every word or phrase in my book, *You Are Salt & Light: Equipping Christians For These Last Days.*

One of the saddest stories in the Bible is the mistake the Jewish people made of not understanding the prophetic Scriptures about the times in which they were living. It is made clear in the New Testament that we are to learn from the many mistakes God's people made as recorded in the Old Testament.

Scripture makes it plain that though the Jewish nation had experienced firsthand the presence of God; witnessed His miracles and blessings; they were deceived by God's clever enemy Satan. They totally missed the incarnation when God became man in the person of Jesus and visited Earth the first time. The Bible states that Jesus came unto His own and His own received Him not.

We don't want to make the same mistake the Jewish people made and not take seriously the prophecies about the spiritual warfare now taking place in our country. It is one of the keys that will equip us all to avoid being overcome and experiencing a major spiritual defeat in these troubled times. It is prophesied in Revelation 13 that Satan will succeed as he works through our superpower position in the world, destroying the biblical standards that people have lived by since the founding of our country. As you examine the fruit produced in our society this last generation you will find this is truer than you can imagine.

America has a strong Christian foundation and has received much Christian teaching, yet we have experienced an

overwhelming increase in the spirit of lawlessness, permissiveness, rebellion and selfishness since World War II. This has happened even though we have more Bible colleges and seminaries;
churches and denominations, Christian books, tapes and videos,
evangelistic outreaches, Christian bookstores, TV and radio stations—more than the rest of the world combined.

So how has the Lord led Barbara and me for the saving of our
family since I had this revolutionary encounter with the Lord; during a period of nearly 40 years that we have seen the standards in
our country deteriorate more than all the previous years since our
forefathers founded America? And sadly during a period when our
country's moral values have deteriorated more drastically in a shorter
period of time since we became the world's greatest superpower than
any society in history, and the trend shows no sign of changing.

The following chapters will reveal how two lay people, like
Barbara and me, who in obedient trust in the Lord, have been
privileged to serve God's Kingdom in ways far beyond our own
expectations and imagination. Now that you have read about the
basis of our spiritual foundation and motivation for building our
spiritual ark, allow me to share the rest of our story.

SEVEN

THREE TESTS

Nearly two years had passed since we had completed construction and moved into our new house. What a joy and blessing it had been for our new family of eight children. Then the Lord began to move in a way that really didn't make a lot of human sense. I began to be led that we should move. Wow, if I was hearing correctly, that was going to be hard. Almost heart breaking for the family.

For two people who had grown up on a farm and now having this new larger home and acreage to accommodate our expanded family, we believed we had the ideal place. Each of the children had found their own special niche and was grateful to God for being a family and having such a wonderful home. We thought this would be our home for our lifetime.

Of our 15 acres of land, we had about 8 acres behind the house that had been cleared and planted in timothy and clover. We cut and had it baled for hay. Then as a family project we loaded each bale on our pickup truck and stacked the hay for future use. We had room to build a barn and have animals.

Barbara loved to mow since she found it was a time of great relaxation. Of course, our place offered her plenty of hours for this much-loved activity. Plus she always wanted everything kept neat, trim and picked up both inside and out. There were plenty of chores for everyone and we enjoyed sharing our home with friends and church members.

The morning I went to tell Barbara the Lord might want us to move she was out on the tractor mowing. When I told her what I thought the Lord's new leading was, she looked at me as if I just hit her in the stomach. I guess, verbally I had. Barbara then turned in the tractor seat and kept mowing as she convulsed in tears. It was several days later before we had more conversation about the subject of moving. There wasn't a lot we could talk about because the Lord had not yet given us any specific details. We kept the subject to ourselves and began seeking the Lord for His direction.

Another thing that happened this same summer was I was led by the Lord to write a book. Let me explain! It wasn't long after my visit in June of 1971 with my brother Charles that I seemed driven by the Spirit of the Lord to do more research and study in the Word of God about end-time prophecy and Satan, along with America's spiritual history. I had to confirm the revelation Charles had shared with me with Biblical facts that were more than just my opinion. It's important for us to understand that even though what appears to be a revelation from God, it still must be tested and confirmed by Scripture. Therefore, I asked the Lord to reveal His prophetic scriptures. I studied them along with commentaries on last-day prophecy and historical books about America's spiritual development.

I soon discovered there are many different points of view on the exact meaning of the symbolic words that describe the characteristics of this "beast" in Revelation 13. Since this was somewhat discouraging for me, I concluded when and if the Lord wanted me to know the exact meaning of all the prophetic Scriptures that describe this "beast," other than the one my brother shared, He would show me. I put away the commentaries and laid the matter before the throne of God.

About a year passed and everything was going smoothly with the family, work and at church when I received another divine message. As I was praying, the Lord spoke in my inner spirit just as He had following the accident that brought six children into our family. He said: "Write a book for your brother about the identity of the "beast."

I had no idea how to write a book or where to begin. Even worse, I dislike writing. In fact, the first time I took the English course in college I failed. If it hadn't been a requirement for graduation, I would have skipped the course. This may sound strange to you because you probably know me best as an author. But my true aptitude is in the field of mathematics and science, which was my major in college.

Knowing I had heard the voice of the Lord, my only thought was to obey His command and I committed myself to writing the book. I had no choice but to trust in the Lord's guidance and perseverance. This was just the beginning of what would be involved in building our spiritual ark. I had no idea this remarkable revelation that identified the "beast" would mean resigning from my job, writing a book, giving up everything we owned except our furniture and clothes, being separated from our church fellowship and that we would move across country. Nor did I expect the enemy would strike where it hurts the most.

Not knowing what was involved in writing a book, I thought it would only take a few weeks. As I began to collect the resources from my many hours of study and research on the subject, I began to put my thoughts on paper. I soon discovered that writing a book is a process, not just an act. It wasn't long before I sensed an inner burden from the Lord to resign from my job as a corporate vice-president of Benada Aluminum. My work was enjoyable and rewarding, yet in spite of this, the Lord gave me perfect peace about making this decision. Though our bank account was limited, the Lord had gifted me with the faith to believe that if we lived on a tight budget we would be able to meet all of our expenses for the next few months.

I well remember the day I planned to tender my resignation because I got so busy I completely forgot. When I got into my car to go home from the office that evening, I suddenly realized something was wrong. When I tried to understand what it was, I drew a blank and pulled out of the company parking lot in a spiritual daze. As I continued to drive home the feeling of heaviness became stronger. I knew I'd done something wrong spiritually and quickly reviewed the day's events in search of an answer. I came up empty. About half way home, the heaviness in my spirit was so intense I had to pull over and stop the car to pray. I asked for the Lord's forgiveness for whatever it was that was causing this heaviness in my heart.

Then just as quick as this terrible feeling came upon me there was a quickening in my heart and a picture of what was wrong became crystal clear. I had become so involved in my job that day, I forgot to resign. I then did something I seldom do, I began to cry. The reason, I had neglected to fulfill my promise to the Lord. Walking in obedience to the Lord's will had become extremely important to me in my relationship with the Lord. My heart was crushed. I immediately confessed my forgetfulness, and just as quickly, the Spirit of the Lord lifted the heavy feeling in my heart. The Lord's presence, peace and joy returned. God is so faithful to His Word that says, *"if we confess our sins,"* He is quick to forgive.

First thing next morning, I turned in my letter of resignation. I had been scheduled to fly to New York, but for obvious reasons the trip was postponed. A few days later I went to work full time as a writer. The first six weeks went smoothly. I studied prophetic Scriptures in Daniel, Matthew, 2 Thessalonians, 1 John, and Revelation on my own without researching what others might say about end-time prophecy. As I studied, the cryptic sentences and symbolic imagery began to make sense. This had nothing to do with my innate wisdom, because the Lord had begun to reveal the hidden meaning of these Scriptures to me. I realize such a statement may raise a few eyebrows, but I knew the Lord's revelations on these prophetic Scriptures were true. I had heard the word of the Lord before, and recognized His voice. You will understand this more fully if you read my book, *You Are Salt & Light*. There I give a detailed description for each word that characterizes this "beast/superpower" in Revelation 13.

Then the unexpected happened. A few months after work on the book Barbara and I experienced a vicious attack from the enemy. It came through some of our dearest Christian friends at church. These were longtime friends with whom we had served, worshiped and fellowshipped. Usually we were with some of these people four to five times a week.

As hard as it was to believe, many of them became our accusers. As I wrote about the remarkable revelation that identified this "beast/superpower" in Revelation 13, I was led to study two books by the Chinese Christian, Watchman Nee. The book titles were, *Love Not The World* and *The Normal Christian Life*. The spiritual principles contained in *The Normal Christian Life* were important to me. I knew Brother Nee had come to know a great deal about spiritual warfare and walking in the power of God's Spirit. In fact I was so struck with these principles I read the book three times, and shared it with the adult Sunday school class that I was teaching at church. That's when the trouble started.

One Sunday after morning worship, I heard that a "secret" elders' and deacons' meeting was underway. I wondered why no one had told me about the meeting, since I was a deacon and should have been notified of any meeting. When I walked into the meeting room, there was complete silence. Then, several fellow deacons and the minister, one of my closest friends, began to criticize me about my teaching. They questioned me about what I had told my class regarding the amount of faith Christians could possess. They then assaulted me with a volley of allegations. They accused me of things I had not done and questioned my motivation for teaching. I was shocked and overwhelmed. I couldn't believe what I was hearing. The confrontation was so heated that those who opposed these accusations almost got into a fight with those who were accusing me. I was saddened and the pain penetrated deep within my heart.

I should point out that the meeting had nothing to do with my revelation that identified the beast/superpower in Revelation 13. I had decided not to teach or discuss my revelation until after my book was finished. I knew before discussing this in public I needed good supporting biblical evidence, not just something that was dependent on what my brother and I had experienced.

What followed this meeting that Sunday became more painful! A few days later the leaders of the church called for and conducted an ecclesiastical trial. They leveled another round of unfounded accusations, then banished Barbara and me from church fellowship. No one explained the rationale for this drastic action except to say they accused me of falsely teaching how much faith Christians could place in the indwelling Holy Spirit to guide our lives. Since it was all based on false statements, and believing this had to be of the enemy, I first planned to boycott the trial. But the night before, while I was praying, the Lord indicated I was to attend the meeting. At first it was rough as they made their many false accusations. Then several men said they should give me a chance to speak though that had not been a part of their plan; those in charge complied.

As I began to speak the Spirit of the Lord fell upon me. Rather than trying to defend myself I was led to share the Spirit's fruit of love and kindness. I spoke, I was later told, for nearly three hours. I don't remember all I talked about for that length of time. I do remember I kept everyone's attention and that I was speaking as a witness for God's nature rather than trying to defend my own position.

During the meeting hardly anyone spoke up on my behalf, but later several of those present told me they had witnessed the anointing of the Lord on me as I spoke. After the trial, the church leaders announced that Barbara and I were to be "marked" and church members were asked not to contact us. That meant we were no longer accepted by over ninety percent of the church membership; although a few did not comply with the decision of the elders ruling and did contact us. Curiously, this happened in one of our basic Bible centered evangelical denominations.

Our new home, once the center of church activities, was pronounced off limits. After the church's ruling, people Barbara and I admired and respected scorned us, and close friends abandoned us. As the days passed we realized what had taken place was not the fault of these dear friends at all. The Lord let us know this had been the work of Satan. We were *battling not against flesh and blood ...*" (Ephesians 6:10).

In the days that followed, the loss of fellowship soon took its toll. Deep depression set in that sapped our energy, and work on the book stopped. For a while, it appeared as if Satan was going to win. The deep-seated awareness that Jesus was in our hearts guiding our way seemed to drift away. He seemed indifferent and remote. It made me feel as though I had lost my way without knowing where or who to turn to.

Then one day the clouds lifted and the peace, power and presence of the Lord returned to us. It brought such joy that I remember it as if it were yesterday. Jane Motsinger, a close friend and sister in the Lord, phoned me. When she called she simply said, "In situations such as you're in we just have to continuously keep our eyes on Jesus and take them off ourselves." Intellectually we knew this was truth, yet for reasons I cannot explain, we had not applied it to our own situation. It is amazing how, when we need to stand firm and spiritually plow though the enemy's barriers, it seems he is able to dupe us.

As this sister spoke, it was as if the Holy Spirit suddenly clicked something within our inner beings. We were delivered. Here was a true spiritual principle that had set us free from the enemy's deadly grip as it has millions of times throughout the history of the Church. I was soon back working on the book.

In a few weeks I finished the first draft and another good friend in the Lord, Gloria Mraz, typed all 650 pages for me. Both of the ladies the Lord used, Jane and Gloria, were members of the church we attended, but had chosen not to comply with the church's ruling.

I was now relieved and elated, believing my days of writing were over, and I began thinking about some of the job offers I had received from several manufacturing companies. I was especially interested in one company not far from where we lived who wanted me as president of their company. However, I was reluctant to respond to the offer because of the leading I had received a few months earlier that the Lord would be directing us to move.

It was a good thing I didn't respond because I soon discovered that my days of writing had only begun. This first manuscript was going to require a great deal of editing, and editing often takes longer than writing. But before continuing to work full time on the book, the Lord began to lead Barbara and me about another crucial area in building a solid spiritual ark for the salvation of our family during these last days.

EIGHT

PREPARATION FOR A MOVE

A s Barbara and I became increasingly aware of the "beast's" system and influence on the morals of our society, we were convicted it was necessary to provide an integrated spiritual education for our children. While our home life reflected a strong committed Christian lifestyle, we were concerned about the secular influence and quality of education they were receiving in the public school system.

By sending our children to a public school at their tender age we believed we were asking them to cope and not be influenced by a humanistic worldview far beyond their ability to understand or evaluate. The question was not could God protect them. The question was, were we being wise and obedient in our responsibility, as taught in Scripture, to raise godly children in an increasingly godless educational system. In our opinion, it was a system that generally had an irrational prejudice against anything supernatural and discounted Scripture and its teachings.

Let me illustrate what I mean by being fair and responsible from a principle I learned early in my business career. Picture a foreman's desk sitting out on the floor in a manufacturing plant. Then, place some hidden cameras near the desk in order to film the surrounding area. Next place a twenty dollar bill on the foreman's desk and have him leave the area. The setup is to film the workers response as they walk by the desk and see the exposed twenty dollar bill. I actually watched such a film. What I observed was about 3 or 4 out of every 10 people would stop, look around to see if anyone was watching. If all was clear, they would pocket the twenty dollar bill and walk away.

The question asked by those who conducted this event was, who was to blame for the action of the workers who picked up the twenty dollar bill? The answer was not to blame the workers, but rather it was the foreman who was guilty. Why? Because a good leader or manager must learn it's his or her responsibility not to put people in a position to be tempted above a level they can handle.

This same principle is taught often in both the Old and New Testament concerning spiritual matters and avoiding temptation. It also applies to our everyday affairs. Take for instance the question of personal debt. Many Christians are often in financial difficulty because they do not understand this principle. Part of the problem comes from being assaulted and seduced daily by professional advertising, beautiful shopping malls and easy credit that make buying "things" beyond our means irresistible. This same principle has also played a major role in the rapid deterioration of our society's moral standards the last forty to fifty years. We have constantly been tempted through the media with moral values that are contrary to biblical teachings.

While Barbara and I were asking the Lord for wisdom and direction in fulfilling our responsibility for the children's education, I was led to Psalm 1:1, 2 that says: *"Blessed is the man who does not walk in the counsel of the wicked or stand in the way of sinners or sit in the seat of mockers. But his delight is in the law of the*

Lord, and on this law he meditates day and night." I thought if this truth applied to adults, it should apply equally as well to young people.

It was this verse the Lord used to convict us to take our children out of the public school system. On one hand, it would have been much easier to ignore this verse; I knew the financial investment for a Christian education for all the children would be huge. On the other hand, if just one fell away from wanting to serve the Lord, or had to struggle at their young age, it would not be worth it regardless of the financial sacrifice. Jesus makes it clear that spiritual values must take precedence over any sacrifice we may have to make that affects the outcome of our children's welfare. If we were to build a solid spiritual ark for our children in these last days, we were convinced this had to be one of the foundational building blocks.

Our view of parental responsibility for raising children was consistent with other Scriptures that outline parental duties. For example, Christians are to teach (Deuteronomy 6:7), to train (Proverbs 22:6), to provide for (2 Corinthians 12:14 and 1 Timothy 5:8), to nurture (Ephesians 6:4), to control (1 Timothy 3:4 & 12), and to love (Titus 2:4). According to Scripture, it's of the utmost importance for Christian children to be educated by born-again believers in a wholesome, uplifting atmosphere. School days should be filled with pleasant memories and character-building experiences based on the Word of God.

I have great admiration and appreciation for young people who have had the boldness and courage to take a stand for Jesus Christ in the face of a humanistic public school policy and opposing peer pressure. At the same time, I am saddened to read how the majority of our Christian young people have been influenced away from their faith by humanistic philosophy taught in our public schools. Since WW II the percentage of our young people who once had their moral values based on the Bible, has, after studying humanistic philosophy, dropped from 65% to 4%.

Barbara and I were in the process of building our spiritual ark for the saving of our family. As we look back we give Him all the praise as we can see that He was leading us so that not a single one of our children would become a sad statistic. Yes, as you continue to read, the sacrifice was huge, but we had the admonition from Matthew 16:26: *"What good will it be for a man if he gains the whole world, yet forfeits his soul?"*

Humanism eschews the reality of a Creator to be worshiped, or a Redeemer who loved us and died to pay our debt of sin in order to reconcile us to God in whose image we are made. Humanism teaches we can, just as if we were a god, decide what is right or wrong. Thus, humanism is the complete antithesis of the Word of God, (see 2 Thessalonians 2:4). A Christian's standards are set by the Word of God not standards of society. Furthermore, Christians are the temple of the Holy Spirit and have been bought at a price (see 1 Corinthians 6:19). This means that out of love for Christ our Lord, our individual will is brought into conformity to the eternal will of God, and that Jesus Christ is the standard for our human life.

In 1972, when we began to seriously think about the children's education, we discovered there were no Christian schools in our community. Therefore, to be obedient to God's Word, we realized we would have to move. I now knew why the Lord had earlier begun to direct our thinking about moving.

In October 1972, Barbara and I scouted several parts of the country that had Christian schools—Georgia, Florida, and Alabama. When we returned from that trip, we had no liberty of the Lord's peace or conviction that we should move to any of these locations. A few months earlier we had traveled to Phoenix, Arizona for me to check out a business opportunity. While there we learned that the Christian community had a strong base of Christian schools. When we returned to Ohio from our southern trip, we sensed a strong feeling from the Lord we should again visit Phoenix, Arizona. The first week in January 1973, along with our good friend John Mraz, we again traveled to Phoenix. We found several Christian elementary schools and a strong secondary school. The Lord gave us complete peace that this was where we were to move. Without delay, we contacted a realtor and began the difficult task of finding what we thought would be a suitable home for our family.

There were several criteria for our home. We knew we would need four bedrooms with two baths. And to ward off Phoenix's sizzling summer temperatures, we wanted a place with a swimming pool for the kids. Further, since we were moving west, our kids, like many young people, would want to have a horse if possible. That meant we would need a property with horse facilities. All this, of course, would have to fit within our financial budget.

By the end of our week's visit, things started to fall into place. We settled in what was then the northern most part of Scottsdale, a suburb of Phoenix (Scottsdale has now expanded much further north). The house we found was a four-bedroom western ranch house, on a one acre lot with a swimming pool, horse stalls and a small corral.

The house had most of what we were looking for. Interestingly, it had been on the market for a while. The reason—the inside decorating was terrible. This helped us when we came to negotiating our price range that we had set at a maximum of $50,000. The fact that the house needed redecorating did not in any way bother Barbara. She quickly saw the property's potential. This is something for which I have no gift. Our offer of $48,500 was accepted, we then flew back to Ohio to put our house and acreage up for sale and to prepare the family for the move to Phoenix.

To leave our new, perfect home we had built for our expanded family we knew would be painful and wrenching for us all. It had been so perfect! Worldly wisdom would have easily convinced us to stay. Though admirable, a move to put our children in a Christian school would not be worth it. However, since receiving the revelation that identified the "beast/superpower" we were determined to follow the Holy Spirit's leading regardless of the pain and disruption caused by leaving our Ohio property. As I looked back, I saw how the three tests we had encountered earlier (I shared them in the last chapter—the leading toward giving up our home, resigning my job and separation from church family) made it easier for us to leave our lovely home in which we had invested so much effort and time. Thankfully, as I've already mentioned, the Lord had been preparing us for this upheaval. In his kindness, He had been leading us for several months about moving.

There was so much to do to get our family ready to move across country, not the least of which was time. In order to enroll the kids and start their second semester, we needed to get to Phoenix by the first part of February. After taking inventory of our household furnishings and those things the children wanted to move, we determined we would need two U-haul trucks. We decided to hold an auction and sell all the other items we didn't need. For example, since there isn't much grass to mow in Phoenix, we wouldn't need our lawn and garden equipment.

I contacted an auctioneer and set the auction for Friday, January 26th. Our plan was to load the U-haul trucks the next day on Saturday and leave on Sunday. This would allow five days for the trip, and with the Lord's help, worse case would be to make it to

Phoenix by Friday, February 2nd just in time for the kids to start their second semester on Monday.

The demanding task of getting cardboard boxes and packing everything began. It is unbelievable how much a family can accumulate. We now had two families to get ready. It took almost three weeks to get everything together in readiness for our trip. Of course, the kids stayed in school during this time so they were not available during the day.

Getting everything and everybody ready went like clockwork. Then to sweeten the pie, the Lord brought a buyer for our home. We signed the papers on the day before leaving. For that we were thankful. Not just because we could put it out of our mind, but we now had the equity to make a down payment on the house in Phoenix, plus have the necessary funds to meet living expenses until I found a job.

We had a relatively short time to advertise our auction. But here again, on the day of the auction the Lord surprised us with a large enthusiastic crowd. It turned out to be a day full of unexpected surprises. The auctioneer was able to generate a happy interest in each item that put people in a buying mood, so much so that people bought items we thought we would have to throw or give away. I remember a small pool table we had purchased for the kids that sold for more than we had originally paid for it two years before. The auction was a lot of fun, and what we sold gave us enough cash to pay for all of our traveling expenses to Phoenix.

As we began to load the trucks on Saturday, several men from church came to help, including the minister, which was a pleasant surprise and blessing, as the results of the trial were still in force. In final preparation to leave, Barbara got the girls busy to help her give the house a good cleaning while we were loading the trucks. The night before leaving we all slept on the floor. On Sunday morning we hooked our pickup truck behind the 24ft. U-haul truck that I would drive (our Australian sheep dog rode in the cab of the pickup), we hooked our 20ft. used travel trailer we had purchased earlier for camping to our 1965 Chrysler that Barbara would drive. The kid's 1967 station wagon was hooked behind the 20ft. U-haul truck that 20-year-old Larry would drive.

We lined up our caravan and headed out of the driveway. But just before pulling out onto the road we stopped, got out of the vehicles and took one long last silent look at our house that was set about a hundred yards from the road. For the last time we stood looking at this beautiful piece of property we had developed. As we each thought about our own special joys and memories, we wept unashamedly, but now we had set our faces as a flint to be obedient to the will of the Lord and we began a new adventure of faith.

Since the children had come to live with us, I recorded our family activities on my 8mm movie camera. This included the property, construction of the house, church picnics, planting the yard in grass and three weeks later when it was completely green, the baling and loading of the hay, putting in an above-ground swimming pool for the kids, and Marilyn's wedding, the oldest of the six children. I filmed every Christmas as Barbara made this a special time for the kids, and much, much more. I continued to take movies of our lives together for many years.

NINE

THE MOVE

Sunday January 28, 1973 our convoy pulled out on the highway to begin the 2,250 mile trek to the "Valley of the Sun" to which Phoenix is often referred. Some friends met us for a late breakfast at a nearby Perkins restaurant. We stopped, ate, and were on our way about 12 noon. For the first two and half hours everything went fine. Then on the east side of Akron, Ohio my truck started to lose power. I quickly pulled off the interstate at the nearest intersection. Barbara wasn't in a position to follow me so she pulled off to the side of the road. Larry was able to follow me.

By the time I found a place to park near the exit, my truck had stopped altogether. We found a pay phone and called the u-haul emergency hot line. (No Cell phones then). Barbara sent one of the girls to find out what had happened. I told her the truck had stopped, but didn't know why. I hoped it wouldn't be so serious we'd have to unload and re-load onto another U-haul.

We looked at a map and found a rest area about 40 miles further west on the interstate highway and decided to spend the night there. The travel trailer was to be our home on the road. It had an extension over the front that would sleep two, the cushioned benches on each side could sleep two more, Barbara and I would sleep on the bed in back, and the smaller children could sleep on the floor.

I told Barbara to go on ahead and when we got back on the road I would meet her at the rest stop. What a dramatic way to start our trip! We were traveling by faith and as some have suggested brute force of ignorance!

The U-haul serviceman arrived in about an hour and found the problem, a faulty alternator. This was Sunday and in those days auto part stores were closed. He didn't think he could get the truck fixed before Monday morning. However he knew of one possibility twenty miles away where he might get the part. As the serviceman took off, I told Larry to go ahead in his U-haul to be with Barbara and the others. The serviceman returned about an hour later. Praise the Lord he had found the right alternator, installed it and we were again on the road. In the meantime it had started to snow.

Barbara is a superb cook. That would be the testimony from many who have been our dinner guests. She loves to cook and thinks of it as a ministry and a way to serve others. Of course our family has been the beneficiaries as it has been her custom to fix a large sit-down full course farm dinner every evening. Now after 53 years of marriage she still does, even though she is now unable to walk (more about this later).

By the time I reached the family at the rest area it was 10:00 p.m. and the blowing snow was coming down hard. When Barbara opened the door she welcomed me with a large hot bowl of home-made chili. Maybe because of the bitter cold or perhaps because I hadn't eaten anything since noon, her chili seemed exceptionally good that night.

We were all exhausted. I'm sure it was partly because of the mental stress of starting such a long trip, the unknown problem that developed with one of the U-hauls, and learning to drive with the responsibility of towing another vehicle. We called an end to our first day and got everyone settled in bed.

The next day we woke to about 4" of snow on the ground. After Barbara prepared breakfast, we again hit the road. For the next two hundred miles, until we reached Cincinnati, the driving was treacherous. The roads were slick and covered with snow. This, plus our inexperience with the vehicles we were driving and towing, made our progress painfully slow. That afternoon we continued on into Kentucky and decided to spend the night at a Holiday Inn where everyone could shower and get a good nights rest. However, Barbara needed more than a nights rest, she needed help. Taking on the responsibility for the needs of the family the way she does, plus driving a full day pulling a travel trailer on the interstate, in a word, she was getting stressed out. I decided eighteen-year-old Brenda, who was studying at Harding University, a Christian college about 40 miles northeast of Little Rock, Arkansas, would be the answer to Barbara's stress problem. That morning I sent Larry and Perry ahead in the smaller U-haul to pick up Brenda for the remainder of the trip to help Barbara drive. The third night we stayed at a KOA camp site near Little Rock. Even though the northern route would have saved us a couple hundred miles I was glad we picked the southern route for the trip. If we hadn't, we would not have been near the University.

Other than a flat tire on the pickup truck on the fourth day, we had no other mishaps. It was two hundred miles from Little Rock to the Texas border and then we faced a long 800-mile drive across the state of Texas. After traveling about six hundred miles, we spent the fourth night somewhere near Abilene, Texas. The closer we got to Arizona, the more excited our family became, particularly as they began to talk about where we would live; we decided to make day five another long day. We picked a small town in west New Mexico on interstate 10 even though it would be another 600-mile driving day. That would leave us about 275 miles for the final day to complete the trip on Friday. We began praising the Lord that the trip would soon be over. And it was now on to a trailer park in a small town in western New Mexico.

On our fifth night, we experienced a major dramatic event. Since my U-haul was the slowest I was the slow poke in our caravan, I left early before the others on the morning of the fifth day. We had picked a place to meet for lunch and I arrived there a few minutes before the rest of them. When Barbara arrived, she began to fix lunch. As the rest of us chipped in to help, we talked through our travels for the rest of the day. Since we still had a long way yet to reach our destination for the night, we decided I would take my lunch and go on ahead. Barbara thought she could catch me by mid-afternoon. I took Perry and Greg with me and we told everyone we would see them when they caught up.

I wasn't thrilled with the idea of Barbara being separated from me and traveling alone during the drive across the desolate areas of western Texas and parts of New Mexico. But we reasoned it wouldn't be more than 3 hours before she caught up with us. I arrived at the trailer park in New Mexico about 7:00 p.m. and hadn't seen Barbara since lunch. I checked in, paid the required deposit and found a spot for the travel trailer and secured a parking place for the two u-haul trucks.

As Perry, Greg and I passed the time in the cab of the truck waiting for Barbara and Larry to arrive, a carload of men drove by. They stopped about 10 yards in front of our truck, sat there for 3 or 4 minutes, and then drove away. I didn't think much about it when I suddenly felt a deep sense of concern. I began to sense this trailer park was not going to be a safe place for us to stay. As hard as I tried to shake it off, the feeling persisted.

As the minutes ticked by, my feelings of concern intensified. When Barbara and Larry arrived about 8:30 I learned she had had a flat on one of the trailer tires. Gratefully a semi-truck driver was kind enough to stop and put the spare on for her. That took an hour. She then decided to stop in El Paso for dinner that lasted yet another hour. Hence the reasons for my long wait in the trailer park.

By the time they arrived, I had left the trailer park and was waiting for them alongside the highway. In my spirit I knew there was danger if we stayed in that town; although what kind of danger I did not know. The next trailer park was 110 miles away in Benson, Arizona. Our fuel tanks were empty and everyone was travel-weary and tired. Yet, I said there was no choice, we had to leave immediately. I knew the Lord wanted us out of that town now. There was danger if we stayed.

We filled the fuel tanks in each vehicle at a nearby gas station and left for the next KOA in Benson. We stayed together and arrived in Benson sometime between 11:00 and 12:00 midnight. I think the anxiety that came through in the emergency of my voice kept everyone awake and alert for that late drive.

The next morning we were all awake early for the last day of our trip. The kids were anxious to get their first look at Arizona. Then something neat happened that morning after we left the danger in New Mexico. This will not have the same meaning to you as it did us, but let me tell you about the Lord's confirmation that it was He who was watching over us the night before and had moved us on to Benson. As we stepped out of the trailer that morning, we were surprised to see, in about two and a half foot letters on the side of one of our U-Haul trucks, the words "Jesus is Lord." When we examined the letters, it appeared someone at one time had put these letters on the side of the truck with masking tape, but the tape had been removed and the letters were no longer visible. However the way we had parked the truck, that morning the unique angle of the sun's rays caused these letters that spelled "Jesus is Lord" to show up bright and clearly visible. No other time had that been the situation.

Here again was another confirmation from the Spirit of God that the Lord was watching over us and that He had been the one to move us on to Benson the night before. However, we still didn't know why, and we didn't find out for a few weeks, which you will read about later. I then recorded this phenomenon with my movie camera.

We were now off to Scottsdale on the last day of our trip. When we arrived we called the realtor to see if our offer on the house had been accepted as we had not heard if everything had been worked out. We were praying that the travel trailer would not have to be our home until we found another property that suited our needs. The news was good. The realtor told us everything had cleared. At first the bank had held off on approving our loan because I didn't have a job or the prospect for one. It was a common practice for people to move to Arizona without jobs to enjoy the weather and in a few months, if they hadn't found employment, leave because they couldn't afford their mortgage. Fortunately we had agreed, if necessary, to make a larger down payment. We were able to do this from the funds received selling our house in Ohio. We were thankful it sold the day before we left.

After receiving this news we went straight to the house. When we arrived, I have to admit it looked pretty bleak compared to the beautiful home we had left. Desert landscaping is drab and unpleasant unless it is well kept. The children too were disappointed, but happy the trip was over. When we went inside we were greeted with an outdated unappealing long shaggy carpet. The kitchen and the orange painted walls were even less appealing. The one good thing was a good size back yard with a swimming pool plus a corral and stables for horses. Barbara, ever the optimist, explained that while it was going to take a lot of work and time, the house had great potential. Her positive attitude brought some comfort. Since the children had seen what we all did with the house in Ohio, everyone started looking forward to the challenge.

Our next task was to unload the U-hauls. We wanted to finish in time to return them the next day, Saturday afternoon. Everyone pitched in and we made it in time to return the trucks on schedule. Of course, unloading was the easy part. Now the arranging of the furniture and unpacking all the boxes had to be planned in such a manner that everything was aesthetic and in neat and clean order. Barbara would have it no other way.

On Monday morning we went to enroll the five children in school. Three were in grade school. Perry was a freshman and Mary a junior in high school. When I went to the office at Phoenix Christian High School to enroll Perry and Mary I met with the superintendent Dr. Crenshaw. He said there was no problem to enroll Perry, but they couldn't take Mary. The junior class was full with a waiting list. My heart sank. We had made the sacrifice of giving up our home and made the long move to Phoenix specifically to enroll the children in Christian schools. Had we misunderstood the Lord's leading?

When I explained to Dr. Crenshaw why we had moved to Phoenix he said, "Bob call me back this evening, I have an idea and should have a definite answer for you then." We immediately began to pray for the Lord's intervention in this situation. I have to admit we were somewhat anxious when I went to a pay phone later that day to call Dr. Crenshaw. When Dr. Crenshaw answered the phone he said, "You must have the Lord's favor. We had a teachers' meeting, and to be fair to them and those on the waiting list, I decided to put your situation before the teachers for a vote. I didn't tell the teachers, but I thought the vote should be unanimous to override the school's policy and accept another student." He continued, "We first prayed and then took a vote. It was unanimous that we should make an exception for Mary." The next day we went back to the school and enrolled Mary with thankfulness to the Lord for His faithfulness.

The equity we received from the sale of our property in Ohio not only provided the funds for a down payment on the house in Arizona, it also provided the funds needed to put the kids in a Christian school and, by living on a tight budget, meet our living expenses for several months.

TEN

THE LORD CONTINUES TO LEAD

S ince God's revelation to me in 1971 with regard to the "beast of Revelation 13," I have been extremely sensitive to His leading. Some of the leadings related to spiritual matters, others had to do with the everyday affairs of life. Some were a divine word as when the Lord said, "Take these six children to raise and build a new home on the property you just bought."

Whenever I have received a spoken word it has been short, direct and to the point. Whatever His spoken word has been, He has always given us the wisdom and direction to complete the task. Another way the Lord has led us is from Scripture like convicting us of the truth found in Psalms 1:1, and 2 concerning schooling for the children.

A third way God has led us is to develop within our hearts a desire to do something. However, this third method requires more caution and patience. We must wait long enough for our emotions to subside before moving forward. I found that what we think may be a leading from the Lord, can just be our own desires.

Barbara and I have experienced all three methods. And all three required prayer to make certain our direction was based on firm spiritual principles that can be confirmed by Scripture.

There have been times when we felt a leading from the Lord and waited for over a year in prayer before we received an answer or release from the Lord to make a final decision. There are other things the Lord has told me are going to happen that go back as far as February 14, 1977 that as yet have not happened.

I will share some of the leadings that have happened since our arrival in Arizona. These will mostly be in chronological order though to complete the story may run over a period of several years.

As I continue, keep in mind that though these leadings from the Lord may appear to be a common occurrence, they have taken place over several years. Most of our life, like many committed Christians, has been to live out the everyday affairs of life. I share these special times in our life in response to Psalms 40:10 that says, *"I do not hide your righteousness in my heart; I speak of your faithfulness and salvation. I do not conceal your love and your truth from the great assembly."*

After we arrived in Arizona on February 2nd I went back to work on the book the Lord had directed me to write. As I reflected on the preceding series of events and our present situation, I had to smile. Eight months earlier I was a business executive with a personal secretary, now I was jobless and doing my own typing on an old mechanical typewriter, stopping to use white-out for every mistake I made. The use of a computer like I am now using didn't exist.

Brenda and Larry went back to college and Barbara began making our house a comfortable heartwarming home. Though she was an expert at doing this, it wasn't an easy task. A brand new house would have been much easier as she first would not have to undo everything. Over the next few weeks, Barbara and I found out why the Lord had led us to leave that small town in New Mexico in such a hurry. We met several people familiar with that town and all repeated the same incredible story. A ring of thieves were robbing the town, and trucks parked overnight in a trailer park were one of their prime targets. The ring's modus operandi was to pull up next to the victim's truck with a semi-truck, clean it out, then head for the mountains or maybe go across the border into Mexico. Do-it-yourself moving vans were the thieves' choice because they were filled with fast-selling household items. One person told me he had grown up in that crime-ridden town and had no doubt that if we had stayed, we would have lost everything. He also said, unfortunately many of those in the police department were involved with the crime ring; therefore, nothing would have been done to solve the crime.

Another man I met confirmed the likelihood of what would have happened. A few weeks earlier this man and his family had stopped at that same trailer park. Like us, they had rented a U-Haul. The next morning they awoke to find the U-haul had been completely emptied. Everything they owned was gone without a trace. How thankful and grateful to the Lord we were that He had intervened and placed a burden in my heart to move on.

Over the next several months our family settled down to a normal routine. We found a church we all liked, the kids were adjusting to their different school environment, and Barbara was busy directing the activities of the home. We also found time as a family to explore the territory around Phoenix. Barbara would fix a picnic and off we would go into the mountains or surrounding lakes to experience landscape and environment that was totally foreign to all of us. Those were enjoyable times.

I completed the second draft of the book, condensed the manuscript to 400 pages, and was confident I was getting close to a finished product. Then one morning after we had been in Arizona for about six months, I awoke to a clear, inner voice of the Spirit of the Lord saying in my heart: "You are to look for a job."

It had been a year since I had left my job in Ohio to write the book. In my heart, I knew I was to now finish writing the book during evenings and weekends and hire someone to type the corrected copy. My first thought about getting a job was to avoid the corporate business world. So I contacted a business realtor to check out the possibility of buying a small business, one that employed two or three people. I found a mobile home repair business that looked promising. I thought since there are a lot of mobile homes in the Phoenix area, I should be able to make a decent living from such a business. I still had a few thousand dollars put aside that would allow me to make a down payment as earnest money for buying the business, all depending on my evaluation of the company's accounting books.

However, when I examined the books, things didn't look right. Their outgoing expenses for materials didn't seem to equate with the many invoices they had recorded for business they had apparently done. I asked for a copy of all of their purchase orders for materials. I was right. The invoiced amounts didn't add up to all the jobs they supposedly had done. This made a huge difference in their reported income. What appeared to be a good business was bogus. Their books had been falsified. I requested my earnest money back and lost any faith that I was to pursue another small business.

My next thought was to consider a career as a real estate salesman. Phoenix was growing fast and this seemed like a good idea. It appeared this occupation also allowed a person to manage their own time and business affairs. So, I enrolled in a real estate school and when I received my real estate license, I was ready to go to work. I remember my first day with a real estate firm. I was there at 9:00 a.m. when the office opened. The manager gave me some assignments that would help me learn the in-and-outs of selling real estate. At first I was comfortable and then after an hour or so I began to sense heaviness in my spirit. By noon this heaviness had become so strong I knew I was not where the Lord wanted me to be. I had made a mistake. A career in real estate was not where I was to work. I walked into the manager's office and thanked him for the opportunity to work with his firm, but I wouldn't be back. I walked out of his office and never returned.

As I reflected back, I realized I hadn't waited on the Lord like I should have. I found there are times He must let us experience something before we can see that we are on the wrong path. In this way we learn from our mistakes. We are not always going to be right every time the first time. There are positive lessons to be learned from mistakes. In order for me to find His direction for work, He had to let me spend six weeks and my money to go through real estate school to reveal my mistake after the fact.

I investigated several other career possibilities, but each time when the door closed, I did not try to pursue it. I then heard about Frank Labriola who had received an SBA—Small Business Admin-istration—loan and was starting a manufacturing aluminum extrusion business near Phoenix. This was the same business I had resigned from in Ohio as Vice President and General Manager. Though this would put me back into the corporate business world, the Lord reminded me of a basic Scriptural truth, that we can be **in** the world, but we are not to be **of** the world. My previous mistakes of trying to find employment on my own allowed me to be open to discussing a job opportunity with Frank.

When I contacted Frank I learned he needed someone with my experience but because of my previous experience he was concerned about my asking salary. He was starting a new company and was on a limited budget. After meeting with Frank and discussing his business plans, I was convicted this was where the Lord wanted me. With this new conviction I told Frank I didn't care what he paid me, even if it was just $1,000 per month. I said I would help him build his company and would trust that if the company was successful he would make it up to me later.

A few days later, Frank called and said, "Bob I have reviewed my financial projections and I can afford to pay you $1250 per month." That was about one third what I was making before moving to Phoenix along with several perks. As a normal rule, most people would have told Frank they would let him know as they would want to keep looking. But I knew I was to accept his job offer and told him immediately I was ready to go to work.

Both Barbara and I were overwhelmed with how faithful the Lord was and how perfect His timing had been. Here was an opportunity in my area of expertise that would let me return to the industry I knew best. Had I not listened to the Lord a few weeks earlier when I received His word to search for a job and if I had stayed in real estate or bought a small business, I would have missed this golden opportunity. When Barbara and I reviewed our budget we discovered that the net income I would receive from $1250 a month was almost to the penny what we would need to meet our minimum living expenses.

In the fall of 1973, I joined this new company called Pimalco. We made our first shipment of aluminum extrusions on November 30, 1973. About a year later Frank called me into his office and made me an officer and gifted me with an interest in the company. By 1975 we had expanded the company's manufacturing facility to include the production of high-tech aluminum alloy aerospace extrusions. This product is one of the materials used to build the structure of the body, wings and tail sections of airplanes. The metallurgical and process techniques required to produce this product are one of the most stringent in the aluminum industry. A company's process technology is continually audited and certified by every airplane manufacturer you supply. This includes Boeing, McDonnell-Douglas, General Dynamics, Grumman, Northrop, Lockheed, Beech, Cessna and others for passenger, transport, military and private aircraft. The metallurgical demands are so difficult that more than 75% of the companies that have attempted to produce this product have failed.

It became obvious to me that the Lord's guidance and wisdom was involved in the business decisions we made for Pimalco. They consistently proved fruitful in manufacturing this difficult product. Over the next several years Pimalco developed into one of the highest-rated and most successful aerospace extrusion facilities in the world. Our success became well-known, and the company became an aggressive buyout target for many larger corporations.

While we were not interested in selling, I had become friends with the Procurement Manager of the Boeing Company in Seattle. One day while visiting him in the early 80's, he told me the new 747-400 airplane was being designed using about 50% of a new high-tech aluminum-lithium alloy that had been developed for the aerospace industry. He said, "Bob, you have got to get Pimalco involved in learning how to produce this alloy" and then called in a couple of their engineers to discuss this issue with me.

When I returned home, I told Frank of my discussions at Boeing and their concern that we develop the process for producing this aluminum-lithium alloy. As we explored the possibility of making this new alloy, we estimated it would cost about 50 million dollars to purchase the equipment, build a casting plant and develop the process technology. While our company had been successful, to consider getting a business loan for that much money was out of our league. Therefore, to obtain this technology to produce this alloy we decided to discuss the various options with five or six of the large aluminum companies that had invested in such research and development.

Every company was open to the idea of working to help get us qualified to produce this alloy. But there was a caveat; each company said in order for them to give us their confidential research and development data, they would need to own an interest in our company. In 1985, Frank (along with me and other members of our management team) decided that if we could obtain the technology to produce this alloy, we would sell up to 40 percent of the company. We choose Alcoa because their offer was the most aggressive and because they were the most advanced in the development of this alloy.

It took about six months for the Alcoa attorneys and the law firm representing our company to work out all the details for the buy and sell agreement. The final agreement consisted of many pages of 8-1/2 x 11-inch legal paper work, measuring about 2 to 2-1/2 inches thick, contained in a 3-inch ring binder.

I happened to be in Los Angeles one day during the time of these negotiations. It was mid-afternoon when I had to drive from one business appointment to another. While I was driving on the busy L.A. freeway system, the Spirit of the Lord came upon me to pray for the negotiations. Up to that point I hadn't thought about the Lord being that involved in the sale of the company. I didn't know what specifically I was to pray for. Nevertheless, I was obedient to the prompting of the Spirit and before long the Spirit had me pouring my heart out to God about these negotiations.

This burden from the Lord to pray lasted throughout my one-hour drive. The next morning I arrived at the office anxious to discuss what had taken place with the negotiations the previous afternoon. I was told, "It is interesting that you should ask." The negotiations had come to an immovable disagreement and everyone was in agreement to bring it to an end and call off the sell/buy of the company. As a last resort, it was decided to contact the president of Alcoa. He was the only one who could remove the roadblock.

After hearing a full explanation of the problem, the president made a decision to compromise on the key point of the disagreement, which resolved the problem in the negotiations. When I asked, "What time did this transpire?" I learned it was at the exact time the Spirit of the Lord prompted me to pray for the negotiations. A few weeks later a similar situation occurred and once again I was away and unaware of a breakdown in the negotiations. At that time all I knew was the Spirit of the Lord prompted me to again pray. Later I learned another deal-breaking problem had arisen and details had been mediated.

As I thought about how the Lord prompted me to pray for the negotiations and saw how they had been resolved, I was convinced it was the Lord's will the company be sold. The decision to sell was ultimately Frank's since he was the majority owner. However, I believe it was God's grace that led us. You will understand why as I continue our family story.

As a part of the final agreement we had to change from the 40 percent we wanted to sell, to 51 percent. Alcoa's Vice President and Chief Legal Counsel called after the negotiations were complete and everyone was ready to sign. He reviewed the contract and said because there was a strong possibility that a large company like Alcoa could have an anti-trust issue with the government if they didn't have controlling interest; their percentage of interest had to be a minimum of 51 percent. We had our law firm examine his statement and found he was correct.

To sell controlling interest of the company to Alcoa increased our selling price considerably. In fact, Alcoa was embarrassed they had not caught the potential of this problem before. This opened the door for them to offer a much higher price for the company. Alcoa also wanted an option to purchase the balance of the company in six years, which we agreed to. At the end of that time they stated that Pimalco was the best operating subsidiary in the Alcoa Corporation and they exercised their option. By then Pimalco had expanded to sales of more than $100 million per year with an employment of more than 600. Frank and I stayed on in executive positions with Alcoa until June 30, 1995, when we both retired.

Though I was only 60, Barbara and I thought my career in industry was over, but the Lord had other plans. Through a series of unexpected events, my retirement proved short-lived. That is another story, which I will pick up later. Let me now return to 1974, soon after I joined Pimalco, and share other events through the years as we continued our walk with the Lord.

ELEVEN

1974 TO 1980

Our move to Arizona was out of obedience to God's Word and to fulfill one of the building blocks of our spiritual ark for the family, namely, having the children taught by Christian teachers in a school with a Christian environment. But a year after we arrived in Phoenix, we faced a crisis that threatened to harm our educational ark.

In January 1974, Golden West Elementary Christian School, the Christian school where our two youngest, Alice and Greg were enrolled (Andrea was now a freshman in high school), sent out a notice that the organization in California that owned and operated the school had declared bankruptcy. Parents were notified the school would close in two weeks. A group of parents called a meeting and decided to try and keep the school going for the next four months in order for the children to finish the school year.

On a business trip to California, I contacted the law firm handling the receivership of the bankrupt company. I met with them and reached an agreement with the lawyer to allow the parents to pay a flat fee per month for the facilities plus pay all of the operating expenses for the complete staff and supplies until the end of the school year in the spring. When I returned, we called another parents' meeting and I outlined the details of our agreement. Everyone was pleased there was no increase in the monthly tuition. And they were particularly pleased they would not have to transfer their children to another school. It was then suggested we form a board to oversee the school's operations until the end of the school year. Several parents immediately volunteered to serve on the board. I was then asked by some of the parents if I, too, would serve on the board. I sensed I should accept. The parents also decided to elect the board's officers. We decided to wait two weeks until the next parents meeting before voting for the officers. In the meantime, one of the individuals on the board began his own campaign for president by calling many of the parents by phone asking for their vote. I don't think the other board members gave it much thought about who should be the president.

At the next parents meeting, the individual who had been campaigning for president was called out of town on business. Because of my involvement with the law firm in California, and because the other individual was absent, a parent nominated me for president to guide the activities of the school until the end of the 73-74 school year. The vote was almost unanimous.

I give these details because we discovered later the individual who had campaigned for the position of board president, plus a small group of parents, had met and formulated a plan to remove any reference to the school being Christian. They also planned legislation to discontinue prayer during our parents meetings. As president, it would have been difficult to override his proposals. At subsequent meetings, he and his group tried to lobby for these changes. Since I chaired the meetings I was able to table the subject without discussion. For the rest of the school year, the few opposing parents often scoffed and tried to disrupt the meetings, even to the point of deliberately making noises during prayer.

I believe the Lord orchestrated this gentleman being absent the night the vote for president was taken. We learned he had prepared a strong campaign speech to give the night of the vote. And since I and the other parents were unaware of this group's plans to overturn and weaken the school's Christian emphasis, he probably would have been voted in. However, the Lord knew what was in this individual's heart and He overruled. This taught me once again that wherever the Lord is involved we need to be ever vigilant. The enemy is always at work in opposition however small the situation.

There is also another reason why I have reviewed what took place at Golden West Christian School. Of course we had to close the school when we had completed the school year. The facilities were quite large and went on the market. Serving as president of the board, the Association of Christian Schools International contacted me about opening a new Christian school in northeastern Phoenix.

In spite of knowing how difficult this would be, Barbara and I were receptive to the idea of starting a new school and we began to plan. We had no facilities or equipment—textbooks, desks, chalkboards, playground equipment, etc. With only two and a half months before the fall term it seemed impossible. How could we locate a facility, obtain the necessary equipment, pull together an administrator and hire a staff in such a short time? There was only one thing to do. For three days we fasted and prayed in an effort to understand what the Lord wanted us to do. At the end of that time, Barbara and I, along with two of the other parents, were led to begin a new Christian school.

Shortly thereafter we began to see the Lord's hand at work. Two years earlier Elroy Ratzlaff and his wife Erma had moved to Phoenix to work as missionaries on the Gila River Indian Reservation. In early June of that year, they believed the Lord was guiding them to return to Christian education. Elroy had served in Christian education most of his life. Before moving to Phoenix he had served 20 years as the administrator of a Christian school in Oklahoma. Elroy contacted me and after our meeting, Barbara and I knew hiring him to help start this new school was ordained by the Lord. However, we still needed a building, teachers, classroom supplies and all the teaching and playground equipment.

A few days after hiring Elroy, I received a phone call from a man in Washington, D.C. He told me he owned a parcel of land in northeast Phoenix. He said the property included a building that had been used for a small private school that had been closed for three or four years, but all the instructional materials were intact. The classrooms were equipped with chalkboards, desks, and chairs. There were textbooks and teaching materials for grades kindergarten through eight. There were playground facilities for small children, plus an acre and a half that could be converted into additional play areas. I did not know anything about this man, and never did learn how he got my name.

When we inspected the property, we found it was ideal for us to start a new Christian school. I signed a two-year lease and over the next two and a half months Barbara and I and others scrubbed, cleaned, painted and refurbished the building and grounds. Elroy and I hired a teaching staff. We named the school Paradise Valley Christian School. The school opened in the fall of 1974 with 34 students.

Through the years, enrollment has grown, teaching and administrative staffs have expanded, and the school now has its own administration building, classrooms, gymnasium and softball, soccer and football fields. As president of the school board, I, along with Barbara, helped direct school operations for the first seventeen years and we still keep in contact. Today the school is one of the major Christian schools in Phoenix (kindergarten through eighth grade). Children attend from more than fifty churches representing many different denominations. The school's web address is www.paradisevalleychristian.org or www.pvcp.org.

For the next two years during evenings and weekends I continued to work on the manuscript of the book the Lord had directed me to write. It rolled off the press in 1975, four and a half years after the visit with my brother, Charles, in 1971. The book was titled *God Reveals the Identity of the Beast.* As the years went by the Lord continued to teach me about these last days and how the enemy would be attacking Christians, especially Christian standards in America. As I learned more about the end-time happenings and the intensity of this spiritual warfare going on in America, I updated the message of my first book.

I was helped immensely in this process when in 1977 Barbara and I, along with our family, began attending Trinity Church. We got to know and appreciate the Pastor, Derald McDaniel, and his ministry. As we became involved in the church, I was elected a deacon and a board member, and later was appointed an elder. In the early 80s, Pastor McDaniel asked me to teach an adult Bible class in the auditorium on the subject of my book.

Trinity was one of the fastest growing churches not only in Phoenix, but in the country. I wanted to do a good job, so to make sure my data was correct, I was motivated to review the material I had and to study and research a lot of new material. The class went well averaging nearly 100 people each session. As is often the case, the teacher comes away with more knowledge and conviction than the students. Though I had written a book and had supporting evidence for my subject, this exercise of teaching a class increased my conviction and commitment to share this message. It also inspired me to update my first book, *God Reveals the*

Identity of the Beast. The new version was published in 1984 under a new title, *The Last Days in America*, referring to America's role during these end-times. The combination of the two titles has sold about 180,000 copies, which I have been told qualifies as a Christian bestseller. These books have been sold without advertising, marketing campaigns or a publicity tour. Only a handful of Christian bookstores in the country have been aware of the book. It has been sold from book racks in grocery stores and through word of mouth as people ordered directly from the publisher. The book is still in print.

After publishing the new book, the Lord continued to teach and inspire me with individual messages for the body of Christ about the end-times. To share these messages, I was led periodically to write a newsletter. To help prepare the way, the Lord sent Gideon Miller, a dedicated servant of the Lord and a friend and minister of the Word of God. He was led to begin an extended fast to help endure a spiritual battle concerning something the Lord was going to begin working through me. He fasted for thirty days. I joined him the last two weeks, eating a meal every third day as I was working full time at the aluminum extrusion company. It was out of that time of fasting and seeking the Lord that I began to write a newsletter.

My first newsletter was published in 1986. Interest in the newsletter increased until there were about 95,000 people receiving it from all parts of the country. I published the newsletter only when I would receive a word from the Lord about a particular subject and I could confirm it with Scripture. How the Lord miraculously provided the funds to print and distribute over 2 million copies of my newsletters, free of charge, speaks of the Lord's perfect timing and faithfulness.

You will recall in 1985, 51 percent of the aluminum extrusion company I helped develop and manage was sold to Alcoa. This was just before I needed a large sum of money to mail these news-letters free of charge. For the years I wrote the newsletter, I had money from the sale of the company. After several years of writing this occasional newsletter, I put the messages in a book titled, *Holy Fear*. It was published in 1992. Copies of this book are still available and being sold through my ministry organization *Christian Life Outreach* web site, www.bobfraleychristianlifeoutreach.com.

It was late in the summer of 1975 when the Lord gave me another word. Early one morning He said, "You are to have another child." I had to tell Barbara and as expected she was surprised. She would be 38 by the time the baby would be born and it would almost be ten years younger than Greg, our youngest. In a couple of months she conceived and became pregnant. Our new son, Michael, was born July 27, 1976. I cannot tell you why the Lord told me we were to have another child. Though, like all of our children, he has been a great blessing. The many people who know us would tell you that Barbara and I are not people who would make up a story like this if it were not true.

Of course the kids were surprised to learn Barbara was pregnant. Especially Alice, who was thrilled! She was the youngest of the six children we took to raise and always had a motherly nature. When Michael was born Alice was eleven and proved to be a great help to Barbara throughout Michael's younger years.

In the spring of 1976 I was asked if I would let my name stand to be the president of the Parent-Teacher Association at Phoenix Christian High School. I agreed and was elected. In June, the word of the Lord came again. He said, "Hold a 'This is your Life' program for the schools Superintendent, Dr. Crenshaw, and Principal, Rev. Buckner and honor them both with a new car."

I had no idea how to plan such an event and no funds to finance the project, much less the funds to buy two new cars. However, in obedience to His word, I set into motion to put this program together. I knew a major part of the program would be the participation of their families, relatives and friends. I also knew this should be a complete surprise for the honored guests. I set the date for December 7. This gave me about five and half months to put the program together. I developed a list of potential participants and asked them to send me pictures and to include a short history and special memories of the two men.

Nearly everyone I contacted cooperated. Within a couple of months I accumulated a wealth of information about both men along with many pictures. In the meantime, I had formed a committee to help me write a script for the program that would incorporate the information and pictures I received.

My plan was to have several family members stand behind the stage's curtain and read an exciting event over the PA system that involved one of the honored guests. I would then bring the participant out on stage and surprise the guest with their presence. I felt comfortable handling the opening and closing of the program but I wanted to get a good Master of Ceremonies with a lot of personality. I contacted a vibrant nationally-known youth speaker who happened to live in the Phoenix area. After reviewing my plan he agreed to MC.

As the weeks ticked by, the details of the program fell nicely into place. However, there was still one major hurdle to overcome. Money to buy the cars! But, as He had done in so many other areas of my life, the Lord gave me the faith to move forward. I contacted a Chevrolet dealer and ordered two new 1977 Malibu Classic cars. Blue, for Dr. Crenshaw and a green, for Rev. Buckner (green and white were the school colors).

I would now have to raise the money to pay for these two cars. I sent out a letter to all of the parents and alumni of Phoenix

Christian High School informing them of the date and the surprise project and asked for those who could to make a contribu-
tion. To make sure we kept it a surprise, they were to send the
checks made out to me and not the school.

I later realized that sending the checks to me may not have
been such a good idea. I knew the funds would not be used for
anything else, but many of those I sent letters to did not know me.
However, I think because of the great respect everyone had for Dr.
Crenshaw and Rev. Buckner and the positive influence they had
had on so many lives, this didn't seem to be a deterrent. By the
time the cars arrived I had received enough contributions from
parents and alumni to pay for both cars with $50.00 left over.

On the night of December 7, 1977, the Phoenix Christian
High School gymnasium was packed with standing room only.
Both men were completely surprised. The evening was a huge success. One of the truly heart-warming memories for me was when,
at the end of the program on behalf of the parents and alumni, I
made the presentation of the gift of new cars. Dr. Crenshaw was
reluctant to accept such a gift. It then came to me to remind him
that the three kings honored Jesus at His birth by bringing Him
gifts. Dr. Crenshaw then accepted the gift of the car.

In the book *Building for Life: History of PCHS—1949-1989,* written about Phoenix Christian High School, I quote from page 117:

> "On December 7, 1977, the Parent-Teacher Fellow-
> ship, under the leadership of President Robert Fraley,
> honored Dr. Loye V. Crenshaw and Rev. Harold
> Buchner with a surprise 'This Is Your Life' program
> for each of them. The program was held in the
> gymnasium which was packed with parents, faculty,
> students, and friends. Then, Dr. Crenshaw and Rev.

Buckner were each presented with a new 1977 Chevrolet Malibu Classic. The honor, thoughtfulness, and
love expressed were deeply appreciated by these men
and their families. The money for these cars was
raised without either man knowing about it, hundreds of people were really able to keep a secret! The
cars, Rev. Buckner's green one and Dr. Crenshaw's
blue one, were driven to school for many years."

I am sharing these details, not in any way to boast about my
faith but as the Scripture reminds us, to always remember the ways
the Lord has led in our lives. Thus I say that every time the Lord
has given me a word or convicted Barbara and me to do something, or informed us about something that was to happen; as we
obeyed it has come true. The Lord is so faithful. He not only gives
us a word about something—He then gives us the faith, wisdom
and directions in how to carry it out.

TWELVE

1980 TO 1995

In 1985, the Lord put into our hearts that we should use some of the funds we received from the sale of our interest in the 51 percent of Pimalco's stock that ALCOA bought that year to buy some land. I explored a couple of opportunities to buy land in Arkansas and Oklahoma. However, our hearts were set on trying to find land near Greenville, Ohio, where we grew up. That area has some of the best farmland in America. Barbara's parents also lived in that area as well as many of our relatives.

The Lord's timing was perfect. At that time, farmland in the Greenville area had been selling for $2000 to $2500 per acre. I don't recall why, but the bottom had dropped out of the price for farmland. We found 160 acres of beautiful farmland that had a farmhouse and barn for $900 per acre. It was located on a major highway, US Route 36, about one and a half miles west of Palestine, Ohio, and 10 miles from Greenville. We had enough funds from the sale of the company to pay cash.

Over the next couple of years Barbara and I, with the help of Barbara's dad overseeing the work, began repairing the buildings on the farm. Barbara's dad and mom lived a short one and a half miles from the farm. We also decided that it would be a good thing to have a two-to-three acre pond built on the farm. We dug out an area where there was a natural county waterway and at the end built a dam. It worked beautifully!

Next, we became interested in building a log cabin that over-looked the pond. Since this was a major project, we began to seek the Lord for His approval. We prayed for a year about building this cabin before the Lord gave us a release to go ahead. For about six months I researched log cabin manufacturers and their design features and discovered there is a great difference in the quality of logs one can use. I concluded it was best to use logs from the mountains in the western part of the country and chose a company called Alpine located in Montana. They use only lodge pole pine timber, one of the strongest and best woods for a log home.

I contacted Dan Studabaker, a relative, and an excellent home builder who lived near the farm in Greenville. He agreed to build the cabin and construction began late 1988 and was finished the summer of 1990. Since Barbara and I live in Arizona, I was often asked during construction how I could be comfortable building a cabin in Ohio without being present to inspect the day-to-day building process.

It's generally recommended when building a new home you should be at the job site often to prevent errors and answer questions. But I had complete confidence in Dan's building experience since he knew a lot more about it than we did. Further, I knew he would be critical and watchful to see that everything was done right. After the cabin was completed, a representative from Alpine visited the site and said it was one of the best built log cabins he had ever seen. Dan did an excellent job, for which we praised the Lord.

In 1991 my brother, Dr. Charles Fraley, took a furlough from the mission field in Africa. Charles told me he had befriended an executive from one of the large organizations in the states that raised funds for mission work in Africa. His friend told him he had left the organization when he discovered that over 70 percent of the funds raised were for plush offices, first class travel, administrative expenses, high salaries, and many perks for those running the organization.

My brother's friend learned that though there are good solid organizations that do good work, like the Billy Graham organization (Charles had worked with Franklin Graham and knew this to be true), many were only sending a small portion of what they raised to the mission field.

That prompted Charles to ask me if I would start an organization where 100 percent of every dollar donated would go to help the poor and needy in Kenya, East Africa where he was doing his mission work. I agreed and founded *Christian Life Outreach,* a non-profit organization that could be used for various Christian projects. The project for helping our outreach in Africa, I named *Help the World/Direct.* Information about this project can be found by logging onto our website: www.bobfraleychristianlifeoutreach.com and clicking on *Help the World.*

Over the years, project *Help the World* has been able to help build hospitals, purchase medical supplies and build health clinics in rural areas. The project has also raised tuition fees for some of the top high school Christian graduates in Kenya to attend nursing school; many of the graduates go on to work in a mission-operated Christian hospital or health clinic.

Christian Life Outreach funded the construction of a girl's nursing dormitory for the nursing school my brother founded and directed at one of the largest mission stations in the world located in Kijabe, Kenya, and it has helped with the everyday needs of the poor, especially children. Other projects started under *Christian Life Outreach* include publishing Christian books and booklets (primarily my own writings), the construction of a Christian Retreat Center in Ohio, and a campaign to save Christian values in America. God's direction in my own writings has been to help equip Christians in America to understand the implications from Scripture concerning these last days.

It had been seven years since we bought the 160 acres near Greenville, Ohio when Barbara and I were contacted by a realtor about 80 acres of land that joined our 160 acres. The land, that did not have any buildings, had been bought a few years earlier by a couple of investors. The realtor told us the investors had developed some economic problems and wanted to sell this land. We were interested since it joined our farm and most of the land was good farmland. We made an offer of $900 per acre (the same price we had paid for our 160 acres) but our offer was rejected; the realtor informed us that $1500 an acre was their minimum price. Of course, he tried to sell us on the fairness of their price but we had no peace about paying that much and forgot about buying this additional 80 acres. We assumed it was not to be.

About six months later, as Barbara and I were having dinner at home in Arizona, the Lord suddenly spoke a word to me that said to offer $1100 an acre for the 80 acres. This came as a complete surprise since we had entirely forgotten about the matter.

When I told Barbara what the Lord had said we both couldn't help but think it was strange. But after a few minutes of discussion we decided I should contact the realtor in the morning and make an offer of $1100 an acre for the land. We, of course, didn't know if it was still available. About thirty minutes later the phone rang. When I answered the phone, I was astonished to hear the realtor, whom we had not spoken to for six months, say, "I am calling about the 80 acres of land I discussed with you six months ago. Would you be willing to pay $1100 an acre for the 80 acres of land that joins your farm?" This was unbelievable! It was the same dollar amount the Lord had told me thirty minutes earlier to offer for that land. I said, "Let me discuss it with Barbara and I will call you back." Of course I already knew what my answer was going to be.

Barbara and I were overwhelmed and blessed by God's faithfulness. He had given us an answer as to what we should do when the realtor called before the call ever came. Obviously we didn't have to discuss the realtor's offer very long, but thought we should wait at least an hour or so before calling back. I called and accepted the offer and the transaction was approved just as the Lord had spoken. This spoken word from the Lord had a special meaning to us in that it confirmed we were in the Lord's will to develop this property; modernizing the farm house, repairing the old barn, building two new barns, a pond and a cabin. Over the years more farmland has become available that joins our farm. This property has now expanded to 610 acres. And though the price of land has increased considerably since the first 160 acres we purchased, each time additional land became available, we had the funds. The Lord's timing has been perfect, allowing us to buy the land debt free. Later I'll share where the funds came from. It involves another major part of our story about a business I started in 1997.

THIRTEEN

1995 TO 2000

On June 30, 1995, Frank Labriola, President of Pimalco and the major stockholder, and I retired from Pimalco. At the time I thought my business career was over, but I would soon discover the Lord had other plans. When the company was sold, ALCOA asked if we would agree to sign a no compete agreement. Frank signed his, but there were a couple of issues with my agreement that needed to be changed in that it was based on my staying with ALCOA as a paid consultant. ALCOA's attorney agreed to obtain the necessary approval for the changes as soon as he returned to ALCOA's home office in Pittsburgh.

However, when the attorney returned to Pittsburgh, he learned he had been transferred to a different division. When that happens in large corporations a person often drops their previous workload and immediately reports to their new assignment. I didn't hear back from ALCOA so my no compete agreement was never signed. I assumed ALCOA was not interested in retaining me as a paid consultant, and didn't give the matter another thought. As I later reflected on this event and what happen afterwards, which you will be reading about, it certainly seemed that the Lord may have orchestrated this attorney's transfer. I will never know for sure.

In late March 1996, about nine months after our retirement, I got a call from a vice-president and friend from Reynolds Aluminum Company. Reynolds had been asked by The Boeing Company to consider entering the aerospace-aluminum extrusion market. This friend asked if I would be interested in forming a joint venture with Reynolds to build a manufacturing facility to pursue the aerospace extrusion market.

He said Reynolds had two extrusion presses and a plant in California that was immediately available. This included several pieces of the necessary auxiliary finishing equipment for aerospace quality extrusions. The normal delivery time for a new extrusion press is about one year, and the cost per press runs from $1.5 to $3.5 million dollars each depending on size. That does not include the cost of a heat treatment furnace, auxiliary finishing equipment and construction of a plant and office.

Although I knew the president of Reynolds, along with this friend, I also was familiar with how quickly management personnel in large corporations can change, so I wasn't comfortable in exploring a joint venture and decided to decline the offer. However, somewhat on a lark, I suggested to my friend that Reynolds sell me the presses and finishing equipment along with leasing me the plant in California, and maybe I would again enter this specialized extrusion marketplace on my own.

My friend at Reynolds said, "In two weeks I have to present my next year's business plan for my division to the board of directors. I will take a few minutes to present your proposal to the board for their approval or disapproval." To my surprise, my friend called after his meeting and said the board had approved selling me all the equipment and leasing me the plant facility in California.

That was in April 1996. I knew it would take several million dollars, which I didn't have, to put a project like this together. Before making a decision or responding to my friend at Reynolds, I began at once to seek the Lord for guidance. I decided to wait on the Lord until He gave me an answer that I knew in my heart was from Him. And more important, I wanted the assurance that God was going to be with me in this project. One morning in August, four months later, I got my answer. On my morning walk I heard the Lord simply say, "I will bless the company."

That was all the answer I needed. Believing this was a word from the Lord, I had the confidence to put all the necessary business ingredients together to start a new company.

I developed a financial *pro forma* for the first five operating years including cash flow projections for the cost of equipment, leasing a plant, plant supplies, operation expense, marketing, office expenses, management, labor, inventory, accounts receivables along with several other items required for such a manufacturing facility.

At Pimalco we paid our invoices in thirty days, which gave me an excellent credit rating in the industry. I had personal funds left from the final forty-nine percent of my stock in Pimalco that was sold to ALCOA, however, before I could move forward, I still needed to raise a few million dollars. To raise this capital I would have to sell about twenty percent of the company to outside investors. Because of the risk involved with any new startup company, I knew this wouldn't be easy. But if I could sell the twenty percent, plus what I could invest, I could handle the rest through credit and make a down payment on the equipment and have the sufficient cash flow needed to get started.

My next step was to take my financial *pro forma* to a securities law firm and sign a contract to work with them to develop a complete business plan that included a securities and operating agreement. It turned out to be a legal document of over seventy pages. I then visited banks and venture capital companies in an attempt to raise the necessary outside investment dollars. After examining my *pro forma* and business plan, there was a definite interest; however, they all wanted a fairly large—about forty percent—share of ownership in the company along with a high rate of interest for the funds they would be loaning to the company.

Since the Lord is my adviser and partner I did not have a sense of His direction or peace in this matter. In earnest prayer I asked the Lord how I was to get the money to finance this new company outside of my own funds and the credit I could get. Then Larry, one of the six children, said "Why don't you offer an interest to family and friends?" I wondered if Larry's idea was from the Lord and began to pray about it. Within a few weeks the Lord gave me a completely unheard of plan. The plan was to offer an interest of ownership to members of my family and friends. I was to place a dollar value on the company and offer to sell them an interest with one quarter of one percent interest being the minimum amount anyone could invest. I was to pay each investor ten percent per year on the amount of money they invested for as long as I had use of their money. Then as the company grew I was to refund the full amount of money each investor made. However, I was to let each investor retain their percent of interest in the company they had bought, even though they were receiving a return of one hundred percent of the full amount they invested.

When I began to let family and friends know of my plan, I was soon overwhelmed. Any new startup company is high risk, but I had more people wanting to invest than shares I wanted to sell. I didn't even have time to let all of my brothers and sisters and friends know about my new company. I later heard some of them were not too happy with me that I hadn't let them know. Each potential investor received a copy of my financial *pro forma* and the business plan which, if they wanted to invest, they had to sign. After receiving all of the outside funding I needed from about forty people, I ceased accepting further investment offers. I actually returned checks received from interested investors.

One has to be amazed at the faithfulness of our Lord. He told me He would bless the company and He did. It was only by His wisdom that I learned how to obtain the funds I needed to start this high-tech aluminum extrusion business. I named the company ALEXCO and made a down payment on the two extrusion presses and finishing equipment from Reynolds. They carried the balance on credit, and leased me their plant in Torrance, California.

My next major hurdle was going to be just as difficult as developing the financial resources to start the company. To produce this high-tech aluminum product used for the framing materials in building commercial passenger, military and private airplanes, requires a high level of process certification from those in the airplane manufacturing business. In fact, I needed a team of twenty or more experienced management and supervisory personnel. Without them I knew I would never be successful in manufacturing and supplying this product or meeting and passing the stringent aerospace quality audits that such a company is continually required to pass.

There were only two other major manufacturers of this product in America, so experienced know-how personnel was scarce. The difficulty of my hurdle would be like trying to put together an all-pro basketball, football or baseball team, with each position being highly critical, yet having only two sources from which to acquire these all-pro players.

I knew assembling a core of experienced personnel could only be done with the help of the Lord. Again, the Lord was faithful to His promise that He would bless the company, and He began to move in a miraculous way.

I was led that I shouldn't try to recruit experienced personnel from the other two companies. I was to let them come to me. I soon began to receive employment applications from some of the most experienced people available for every department. Some people might say it was because of the good reputation I had developed with the Pimalco Company. However, I knew it was the Lord that moved in people's hearts. For one thing, in order for them to work for my new company, they would have to leave their home and work in California during the week and return home on weekends. Also, I let everyone know I would not pay them more than they were currently making as I decided it wouldn't be ethical to try and buy my management and supervisor staff.

However, none of these things seemed to be an issue with any of the applicants. Before long I had assembled a group of the finest and most experienced personnel in the industry to produce this difficult aerospace quality aluminum extrusion product. ALEXCO officially began on March 1, 1997. Barbara and I traveled to Torrance, California, a suburb of Los Angeles where the plant was located, to rent a large apartment and we furnished it for our management employees to live in during the week. Within five weeks we had installed several additional items of finishing equipment necessary for producing aerospace aluminum extrusions and converted the extrusion press in this plant to produce the same.

Because of my past relationships in the industry, I contacted Boeing and they sent in a team to certify ALEXCO to supply them aerospace extrusions and soon after other buyers of this product followed. On April 21 we began production. Within three weeks the company had received enough business to operate at full production 24 hours a day, six days a week. This was unprecedented. I then began to look for a location in the Phoenix, Arizona area where I could build a new plant. This was where my family and most of my management and supervisory personnel lived. My next major hurdle was raising about two million dollars to build a new office and plant to ALEXCO's specifications to house the manufacturing operations.

I soon discovered that even if a financial institution was interested, they all wanted my personal financial statement to guarantee the loan necessary to build a new building. That presented a problem. Even if my personal financial statement was strong enough, which it wasn't, and since I was already in my sixties, I had made a commitment to Barbara I would not sign any personal guarantees to start this business. I knew if I did, it could potentially mean the loss of our house in Arizona and the farm in Ohio along with our other assets. I reassured her at our ages I wouldn't take such a chance.

However, I was told by several people that no financial institution would finance a two-million dollar manufacturing building to my specifications without any collateral to guarantee the loan; the risk was too great. I could walk away at anytime and they would be stuck for the full cost. Not only that, since this would be a building built to my unique specifications for producing aerospace extrusion it would require additional expense to modify in the event it had to be sold or leased.

Again I was dependent on the Lord to intervene. An industrial park where I knew some of the people, but had originally turned me down unless I would sign a personal guarantee, called and asked me to come in for a meeting. As we began to discuss construction of a new plant, they said they had changed their minds. They would lease me the acreage and finance the building per my specifications. However, they would keep ownership and lease it to me for a long term and would not require my personal guarantee.

I knew immediately this was an answer from the Lord. It solved the commitment I had made to Barbara. I signed the lease, engineering drawings were completed, and on July 25, 1997, I broke ground to begin construction for my new plant in the Lone Butte Industrial Park in Chandler, Arizona, a suburb of Phoenix.

By January 1998, this new plant was finished. I began installing in this plant a third extrusion press I recently purchased along with the second press I had originally bought from Reynolds. A new state of the art heat treat furnace and other manufacturing equipment was installed and this new facility was soon operational even though I continued to operate the plant in California.

ALEXCO'S office and manufacturing facility.

At the end of 1998, nineteen months after ALEXCO began production; our business had been so successful the company was debt free. As God had promised, He had truly blessed the company.

When the attack on the World Trade Center and the Pentagon occurred on September 11, 2001, it had a major effect on the airline companies. This in turn was reflected in the decreased production of new airplanes. Within weeks, suppliers of materials to the aerospace industry saw a significant downturn in their business, including ALEXCO. However, we were debt free and in excellent financial position to weather any business downturn. Even though business conditions were still slow, a year later I began to sense I was to expand ALEXCO's capacity. I did not receive a direct word from the Lord to expand, but had a strong gift of faith that I should move forward.

If I was to expand and increase our market capabilities, I knew I needed a much larger extrusion press. I also knew it would be a huge expense. In addition I would have to expand our plant and add several pieces of auxiliary equipment.

I had my engineering staff develop the specifications for a new extrusion press that was about fifty percent larger than what we had and was capable of producing high-tech aluminum extrusions. Next, I got quotations from major press manufacturers. It was strange, but in my heart I developed a price I should pay for this press regardless of what any company quoted. It was from one to one and a half million dollars less than the quotes I received. Yet I knew I was to stand firm on my price.

I began to negotiate with one of the world's premier manufacturers of extrusion presses. After a few discussions they agreed to lower their price about $400,000 dollars. Because of the faith the Lord had given me to stand firm on my price, which was a million dollars below their bid, I said no.

We continued to negotiate and they continually kept calling back to their home office to get approval for a lower price. Eventually they got within $50,000 of my price. They said this was their final price. The two representatives in the meeting were told not to call anymore. They said they couldn't believe they ever got approval to go as low as they had. But I still had the faith not to budge.

They couldn't understand my position and didn't know what to do, nor did they want to leave without getting a purchase order from me. This would have been a major embarrassment for them to return to headquarters without a purchase order. I knew this was the best extrusion press on the market. But in my spirit I still felt I should stand firm in my price. You may think I was being too arbitrary. However, it was a matter of obedience to do what I knew in my heart I was to do. While I had not received a direct word from the Lord I was given the faith to believe I was being led by the Holy Spirit. If I was, then the important thing for me was to be obedient, even if it meant not buying the press and not expanding.

The two men from the press manufacturer asked to be excused from the meeting. When they returned several minutes later they, on their own initiative, reached a decision to offer two additional options on the press for only $50,000, the dollar amount of difference in the negotiated price.

I liked their idea and sensed in my spirit a release to move forward with the purchase. However, before doing so, I wanted to double check with Bob Jackson, my VP of operations and highly qualified equipment engineer, on the value and use of these two options. He acknowledged their value. My plant manager, Roy Hurlburt, said he would hate to have a press of this caliber without these two options. It would be like buying a fine car without having power windows and air-conditioning.

I asked the Lord once more to give me the assurance that this was what He wanted me to do, or <u>cause something to happen so I would know I was not</u> to move forward with this expensive purchase. Since I heard or received nothing, I signed the purchase order in February 2003.

When word got out I had bought a new press, the rumor mill in the industry started buzzing. Even though the demand for these high-tech aerospace extrusions was starting to recover, it was still slow. The size of this press was going to double our capacity. People in the industry were asking, "What does Fraley know that we don't?" Of course I didn't know anything others didn't know, except I was given the faith to follow the guidance of the Holy Spirit who knows all things.

When the war in Iraq started on March 20, 2003, the aerospace industry took another hit. I wondered if I had been wrong in sensing I was following the guidance of the Holy Spirit to expand our business. In April I called the press manufacturer and asked if I could, temporarily, and without any penalty, put my order on hold. Other than covering their initial engineering cost, which would be minimal, they approved.

I began to seek the Lord about canceling or buying this press, but I didn't get an answer. A few months went by. I hadn't done anything with my order when I heard that China had placed an order for thirteen presses from this manufacturer. And all were sold at nearly full price. I was also told at the time I purchased my press that my order was the only one they had on the books. Yet I was still in a quandary as to what I should do. Any expansion requires more than double the cost of just the press. There is auxiliary equipment to buy, the cost of installing a 700,000 pound piece of equipment—the weight of the press—plus the installation of high-powered hydraulic pumps and electrical equipment to operate the press. Then there is the construction of several thousand additional square feet to house the press, and several hundred thousand dollars for tooling. I could go on with the cost of several other miscellaneous items. But the point is, I continued to pray because I wanted to hear from the Lord before I released the press manufacturer to make the press.

In early October the press manufacturer called and gave me one more month to make up my mind. If I did not release the press by then, they would have to cancel the order. I continued to pray. Then, just a few days before the thirty-day deadline, I woke up about 3:00 a.m. and was led to go to our family room. I sat down and started reading my Bible that I keep by the table beside my chair. While I was reading, the Holy Spirit suddenly urged me to pray about this press. As I was praying, the Lord said, "I saved you one million dollars, what are you waiting for?"

I discovered later the manufacturer was willing to negotiate, going so low, because they did not have one order on their books for an extrusion press. I didn't know this, of course, but the Lord did. I truly believe this was one of the reasons why I was motivated to expand our operations when I did. The next day I called the press manufacturer and released the order to produce the press. It turned out to be one of the best things the Lord did in directing me to expand the company.

It took a good ten months to manufacturer the press, another month for shipping and about two and half months to install the press. By then we had expanded the plant and purchased all the auxiliary equipment. It was late December 2004, thirteen months after releasing the purchase order, that we ran our first product on this press.

With any piece of large complicated equipment it takes a good eight to twelve months to debug, fine tune and train your personnel before it's a good productive operational part of your business. That took a good part of 2005. By then the demand for aerospace high-tech aluminum extrusions had turned around and we were able to book the business to load this press. The highly efficient and productive quality of this press makes it one of the best in the industry.

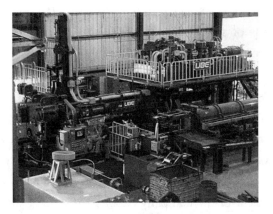

ALEXCO'S Large Extrusion Press with Operator

Only the Lord knew what was to take place in the aerospace industry. I believe it was His guidance that led me to double our capacity. Today ALEXCO is one of the major suppliers in the world of high-tech aluminum extrusions to the aerospace industry. You can read about the many facets of ALEXCO on our web site, www.alexcoaz.com. The Lord is so faithful. All of the praise goes to Him.

In 2004, ALEXCO was selected by a large manufacturer of regional jet commercial aircraft to receive their 2003 Raw Material Supplier of the Year Award. This was in competition with all of the aircraft manufacturer's material suppliers throughout the world. ALEXCO became the first aerospace aluminum-extrusion company to be certified to the new, more stringent aerospace quality certification requirements. This made a huge statement to the entire aircraft-manufacturing industry about our management, supervisory, and production capabilities.

ALEXCO was also selected as the U.S. Small Business Administration's 2005 Region IX Subcontractor of the Year. There are ten regions in the country, and the competition for this prestigious award is keen. To be selected as one of the top ten out of over tens of thousands of small businesses in the U.S. is quite an honor. ALEXCO was honored during the Small Business Administration's Expo 2005 event, held at the Hilton Washington Hotel in our nation's capital. Any company with less than 500 employees is classified as a small business. ALEXCO has around 200 employees.

In order to be considered for this award, each company is audited and undergoes a comprehensive evaluation. After which they receive a written report on ten key categories. The first is management, which is an assessment of the company's ability to organize and utilize its own resources to ensure accomplishment of their business objectives.

Small Business Administration 2005 Region IX
Sub-Prime Contractor of the Year Award

The other nine categories, without explanation, are (2) Financial Stamina and Controls, (3) Labor Relations, (4) Customer Interface, (5) Technical Capabilities, (6) Resource Utilization, (7) Cost Performance, (8) Delivery Performance, (9) Quality Performance and (10) Overall Evaluation.

Each company is graded on a ten-point scale in each category. A grade of 1 is considered satisfactory, 2 or 3 is good; 4,5 or 6 is excellent; 7,8,9 or 10 is superior. ALEXCO received a 10 in *every category*. This is a reflection on the quality of personnel the Lord has blessed us with. When President George W. Bush spoke at one of the Expo's luncheons, he said the small-business sector of the American economy is one of our country's great strengths and is at the heart of America's economic growth.

A cover article about ALEXCO in the June, 1998 issue of *Light Metal Age*, the international magazine of the light-metal industry, included the following. "Fraley has a deep concern for the welfare of others, as is evidenced in his company's bylaws: A minimum of 10% of before-tax profit is annually given to help the poor and needy."

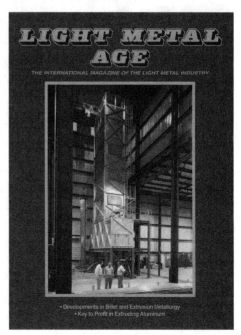

Front Cover of Light Metal Age, June Issue 1998, Showing New Heat Treat Furnace with Perry Fraley (left) Bob Fraley, and Bob Jackson

The Lord's development of ALEXCO has given me the funds to support my brother's many project ministries that he developed to help the poor and needy in Kenya. Over the years, ALEXCO, working through *Christian Life Outreach/Help the World,* has been able to help fund the construction of hospitals, health clinics in Africa's bush country, a girl's nursing school dormitory, provide medical supplies and help fund a dormitory for a Christian grade school near Nairobi, Kenya.

In addition to our outreach in Kenya, we have supported many Gospel ministries in the U.S. We have also been a strong supporter of Christian education by helping Christian schools in the Phoenix area. The success of ALEXCO has allowed us to expand our Ohio farm to 610 acres. As more land became available next to land we owned, and as funds became available, we were able to buy this additional land without going into debt. To find out more about our various ministries, check my web site at www.bobfraleychristianlifeoutreach.com. For more specific information about projects in Kenya, East Africa, go to our home page and click on *"Help the World Direct."*

Soon after I developed ALEXCO, a high school and grade school facility near our farm in Ohio was consolidated with another school. Consolidation of schools had become a common practice in farm communities. When we heard the school property was vacant and was going to be auctioned, Barbara and I wondered if the buildings could be used for a Christian ministry. We agreed to put out a fleece before the Lord by both of us writing down a maximum dollar amount we would bid for the property. When we shared what we each had written it was the same dollar amount—$50,000! We went to the auction with the agreement that $50,000 was our maximum bid for the property. Though our dollar amount was low, we were successful in buying this school property that consisted of a high school building, and grade school building with better than six adjoining acres.

As we prayed for the Lord's direction in how we were to use this property, we were led to completely remodel the facility and convert it into a Christian retreat center. I contracted with an architectural firm to examine the condition of the facility. The high school building was built in 1927 and the only thing salvageable was the outside brick shell. The architectural firm engineered a complete renovation and worked with us to design a modern building for a retreat center.

I again contacted my relative—Dan Studabaker—the one who built our log cabin, and hired him to oversee the remodeling project that began in the spring of 1999. Praise the Lord, from the success of ALEXCO, we were able to assist in providing funds for this project along with some of Barbara and my personal funds. By hiring a full crew and using good sub-contractors, the renovation and a complete remodeling was completed in about a year.

It took 138,000 feet of new electrical wiring and a new furnace and air conditioning system with all the duct work. We installed all new plumbing that included a water softener and three large commercial hot water heaters. We renovated the kitchen with new equipment and the dining room. Every room in the building was gutted and replaced with new dry wall and furnishings. We modernized the restrooms and added two more, each equipped with showers. All of the classrooms were partitioned and converted into sleeping quarters.

Barbara designed and equipped one large room as a relaxing lounge with a fireplace, player piano, game table, etc., as well as supervising the decoration of the entire facility. We refinished the gymnasium, the basketball floor, the seating, and equipped the stage with new curtains and the auditorium with a professional

PA system. That was ten years ago and people still rave about the appearance of the facility.

Our new retreat center is equipped to sleep sixty-four people. All meals are prepared farm style using Barbara's recipes and meal plans. In addition to the gym, there are two classrooms for meetings. The recreation facility is equipped with a pool table, two ping pong tables, three pianos, a player piano, an organ and a basketball court that can also be used for volleyball. Our farm is about one and half miles away and is equipped with a fire pit for cookouts and camp fires, hay rides and hiking, and a two and a half-acre pond stocked with fish.

The mascot of the high school athletic teams was a golden eagle; therefore, we decided to name the facility Golden Eagle Christian Center. We had an artist paint a golden eagle in the center of the gymnasium floor with the verse from Isaiah 40:31 underneath the eagle that says: *"But they that wait upon the Lord shall renew their strength; they shall mount up with wings as eagles; they shall run, and not be weary; and they shall walk, and not be faint."*

The retreat center opened in the summer of 2000. Our son Greg, who has his masters of Divinity from Southwest Baptist Seminary, and his family moved to Greenville, Ohio to help develop the center. The retreat center soon became a favorite for churches, Christian groups and pastor week-end retreats for all Christian denominations within one to two hours traveling distance.

The Center's huge success is due in a large part to Barbara's overall direction. She has used her gifts of hospitality, food preparation, plus her fidelity to cleanliness and comfort to create a pleasant heartwarming environment. Because of this the majority of weekends are booked every year and after ten years of operation, the Center is still as clean as it was when it was first opened. The International Conference of Athletes In Action U.S. basketball team, and coaches from various parts of the world, held their retreat at the Center in the fall of 2009. The center received their highest recommendation and they plan to return January 2011.

The Lord has truly blessed us with a wonderful staff to operate the Center with a talented maintenance man to care for the overall facility. Our daughter-in-law, Gina, Greg's wife, now handles the bookings and contracts with the various groups.

Golden Eagle Christian Center Showing Front of Building,
Small Group Discussion, Lounge and Gym

To know more about our Christian retreat center visit web site www.bobfraleychristianlifeoutreach.com and click on *Golden Eagle Christian Center*. It is located in the small town of Palestine, Ohio about 8 miles east of Greenville, Ohio on U.S. Route 36. Brochures with full description and pictures are available from *Christian Life Outreach*.

FOURTEEN

A LOOK AT FRUIT

I had my seventy-sixth birthday in 2010 and Barbara had her seventy-second. Before I share my next chapter, "My Last Major Calling," I want to jump ahead and share an event that happened during our morning worship service on Mother's Day, May 9, 2010. On that Sunday morning our pastor, John McGovern of Trinity Church, asked Barbara to be the speaker for the morning worship service.

There is something about Barbara she would rather I didn't tell you. It's also not easy for me to tell you because it requires me to focus on a painful event in our lives. About twenty years ago, while Barbara was bowling in the women's church league, her foot got stuck on the alley when she released the ball, and it caused her to pull something in her neck. Several days later she noticed a slight loss of control in that leg. As the months passed, she had increasing difficulty with her balance and control in the movement of both her legs.

Within a couple of years, there were times Barbara was using a cane to keep her balance. We prayed daily for the Lord to heal her of this strange malady, but like many of the psalmists who asked God for an answer, He was silent.

Barbara went to Mayo Clinic in Scottsdale, Arizona and underwent an exhaustive examination. The results proved to be inconclusive. However, the doctors suspected she was developing MS (Multiple Sclerosis). Over time, her legs continued to weaken and our church family as well as our immediate family, and Christians from around the country, began to pray for her healing.

Barbara was examined by some of the best neurologists including the Barrow Neurological Institute located in Phoenix, Arizona. Although their diagnosis was never conclusive, they suspected she had chronic progressive Multiple Sclerosis. This is a slow but progressive type of Multiple Sclerosis that affects the nerves and inhibits communication to the muscles disallowing them to do what you want them to do. About ten percent of those who have Multiple Sclerosis have this type and there is no treatment or suggestions for improvement. About eight years ago, limited in the use of her leg muscles as they became so weak she was unable to walk, Barbara became confined to a wheel chair.

About one and a half years ago, as her leg muscles even grew weaker, she could no longer lift her leg to get into bed or into a car. This has become one of the things I do in love for her. Although the Lord has not healed her, the testimony of her life over these years is a powerful witness of how the Lord has equipped someone to be strong in their weakness. Her bubbling personality has not changed. Her quick wit and good humor that make people laugh and feel good about themselves is still the same. Her gift of hospitality hasn't changed. At any gathering she is still the one person people want to be around. And kids still think it's fun to be with her. When you ask how she is, her usual reply is, "I am terrific." Even though she is sitting in her wheel chair or an electric cart, her attitude is always positive and upbeat.

THE BLESSINGS OF OBEDIENCE

While it's physically taxing, and now takes her twice as long to prepare a meal, she continually invites people for lunch or dinner. Perhaps not as often as before she became handicapped, but she still enjoys sharing her gift of hospitality. Over the recent Christmas holiday, we entertained forty-five people for dinner on one occasion and on another there were over twenty for dinner. Some people wonder why I'm not more aggressive in discouraging her from adding this kind of stress and labor to her life. They would understand if they knew how much enjoyment she receives from serving others. At times, I have to admit her entertaining presents something of a dilemma for me. However, she considers the stress and tiredness that follows after she has prepared a large dinner is a small price to pay for the joy she receives by serving others. It would bother her more not to be able to share her gift of hospitality.

One of Barbara's joys was to participate in athletic activities. She was once a good athlete and loved supporting our three boys and their friends in their athletic activities. This, along with being a super homemaker in raising our family, left her little time for her own athletic interests. She was looking forward to some free time when the children were grown to once again involve herself in her favorite outside sports. Of course, her condition has precluded this.

As a prelude to sharing the transcript of Barbara's discussion during the Mother's Day church service, you need to know there were no beforehand preparations. The discussions were spontaneous, including our boy's responses. None knew what questions they would be asked. Barbara could have picked all nine of our children to answer questions. But all nine would have been too many. Therefore, she picked the four boys including Larry, one of the six who was seventeen when he came to live with us after their parents were tragically killed in an automobile accident in 1969.

THE FOLLOWING IS THE TRANSCRIPT FROM THAT SUNDAY MORNING

PASTOR JOHN McGOVERN: The Fraley's were part of the group of people who joined this church shortly after it began. Several of their kids were raised in this church. I'm happy a few of them are here today. Of course, they're not kids any more. They're adults who have grown into men and women of God. The reason is they had a foundation in the Word of God because a mother and father decided that "as for me and my house, we will serve the Lord."

It's tough to be a mother in this day and age. I'm glad, therefore, that we have women of God in this church like Barbara Fraley who has faithfully walked with our Lord. And so, I've invited Barbara this Mother's Day to come and speak to us. She didn't want to do it alone, and brought her four sons, Greg, Perry, Larry and Michael. They will share a few thoughts about growing up with their mother.

BARBARA FRALEY: This is only the second time I've done something like this. Though it's a little scary, I've decided to make this a panel discussion and invited my four sons to be a part of it. When Pastor John asked me to do this, I sat down with Carmen (Carmen is a lady in our church) and said; Carmen, I can't do this. What do I talk about, what do I say? Carmen said, "Just look at the fruit…." [Pointing to her boys, Barbara says] Here are four of the fruit. Take your pick. One of the boys interjects: Some of us are weathered fruit, some of us are better fruit...but we *are* fruit.

BARBARA: They are definitely not perfect and I was not a perfect mother.

GREG: What!

BARBARA: I know, surprising...right? Well, Greg was the second child, and probably was as perfect as a child could be. I could take him to Bible Study for two hours and he would sit and play with his little Fischer Price barn (my daughter-in-law wonders how that could have happened, because hers wouldn't do that). Greg was good.

Larry our oldest son came to us when he was seventeen. I have to admit it was a little difficult to have a teenager when I was only thirty-one. Larry was raised by godly parents, so raising him was easy compared to what a lot of people go through with a seventeen-year-old teenage boy today. As many of you know, Larry's parents were killed in an automobile accident. Under God's direction we took him and his five sisters to raise. Our son Perry was eleven at the time. Nine years later Greg came along, and nine years after that, Michael came along. Those three boys think they are an only child, and I don't let them know otherwise.

I don't want this to be a "Praise Mom Day," especially this mom. I want it to be a reality of what we experienced in the day-to-day experiences of raising a family. There're a lot of reality T.V. shows. Well, our reality is our children were pretty much raised the way my husband and I were. We were farm kids. You had to work hard and mom was the boss of the household. That's just the way it was. If you check your Bible, mom and dad are supposed to be the boss. However, I've noticed this is often not the case in today's society. But, I'll go out on a limb this morning. I have three daughters-in-law and a daughter here this morning. If you have any questions for them I'll let them speak for themselves. A lot of you here this morning are single moms, and I would not want to trade that job for anything. I pray that you have some male presence in your child's life. Without my husband's commitment to our family and the things we believed in and taught it would have been tough without my dear husband's help and support.

Our kids were raised in a Christian home and went to Christian schools. Some people might call our family "overprotected." But look at the fruit of this "overprotectedness." They married Christian mates. They all have good jobs and they didn't end up sitting in corners sucking their thumb because they were overprotected from life. Each has managed to do well in the business world and they are raising their kids similarly to their own up-bringing. Our family now numbers sixty-five with two more on the way.

One thing I want each of my boys to answer (Barbara speaking to the four boys) is why didn't you rebel in your teen years? What was it that kept you from rebelling? People say it's normal for a child to rebel in their teen years. I say that is a lie from the enemy. They do not have to rebel. Larry, you answer first. Why didn't you rebel?

LARRY (now age 56): I was afraid! (A couple of the other boys chimed in "very afraid," "amen" and there was some laughter). The reality is I've been blessed to have had a lot of spiritual guidance. One of the "ditties" I remember hearing early on from my former pastor when I was about thirteen was, "There are no big decisions in life." The explanation is, big decisions end up being decided by how we choose to make the little ones. I just felt there was nothing good to come from rebellion. Of course, I wouldn't say I never rebelled a bit. (Barbara interjects: Not to the point where we had to beat you!) (The congregation chuckles.)

MICHAEL (now age 34): Yeah, I'm right there with Larry. I was scared to death to rebel. It wasn't anything I even thought about doing. I had the "HOLY FEAR" the Bible talks about. I had it. (Barbara interjects: "Still has it!") In my high school years I hung out with a bunch of friends who were good Christian kids at a Christian High School, but who still did a lot of things I was not allowed to do. I didn't see an "R" rated movie until I went to college. That was like; whoa! (Perry interjects: "You weren't supposed to do that." Michael responded, "Yeah, I know.")

And we had the same restriction with music. I remember Dad telling me specifically what stations I was allowed to listen to. And if I was going to have a car, and he was providing it, this was the music I was supposed to listen to, and of course I was tempted to change the station. I'm not going to say I never did. But when he found out I was listening to the wrong station, I got in trouble.

This fear I am talking about wasn't a negative fear. I love my parents to death, and because I loved them, I didn't want to disappoint them. And this kept me out of a lot of trouble that other kids were getting into. Just having parents and a mom that cared for me made me want to obey them.

I now coach high school football at a Christian High School, on the side from my regular job, and I've noticed how many kids have no one to be accountable to. They are allowed to do whatever they want, and listen to whatever music they want to. When I hear the way they talk, I wonder, where is the accountability of the parents? I was afraid to rebel, partly because of the discipline in the home, but also because of the love and respect I had for my parents. I did not want to hurt or displease them. I think that kind of fear or respect holds true if we truly love God.

PERRY (now age 52): Several years ago I was listening to Dr. Dobson on *Focus on the Family* who was talking about something that had taken place in a school. This school had grade school kids that had a fence about eight to ten feet tall around their playground. During recess the kids would go out on the playground and play all over this entire playground and they would have a blast. But then some parents said, "These kids look like animals stuck in cages. It's horrible, and we've got to get that fence torn down." So after filing grievances and going to the school board, the parents got their wish; the fence was torn down.

Guess what happened when the kids went to play at recess? Because there were no boundaries, they quit playing all over the place and instead huddled together in the middle of the playing field. They feared others coming in to get them. They didn't know where the boundaries were.

The thing I remember as a kid was that I had boundaries. And, as Michael said, Dad and Mom both let us know what those boundaries were. The interesting thing was I had a blast when I kept within the boundaries. That's what Mom accomplished. She made it fun as long as I stayed within the boundaries. If I stayed in the boundaries, life was good. If I got outside the boundaries, life was bad. It was that simple. So, after a while, you learned to stay inside the boundaries.

As a Christian parent I've really tried to let my kids know where the boundaries are. And I let them enjoy the time in the boundaries. My mom spent a lot of time making sure our family enjoyed living within the boundaries. Whether it was taking picnics out to Fountain Hills, or it was having parties that were over-the-top. If you've ever been to one of Mom's parties, they are over-the-top! I'll never forget my 7th birthday. It was one of the most incredible things in the world. Those are the kind of things to consider when raising our

children. As Christians, we are not condemned
to a life of misery. The joy of the Lord is abun-
dant. At the same time, the Word of God gives
us boundaries. Who are those boundaries for? It's
not for God. God doesn't put those boundaries in
place to limit us. He puts those boundaries in place
to protect us.

BARBARA: Amen.

GREG: Nice Sermon…

MICHAEL: …And you're not even the preacher!

BARBARA: Yeah, you're [speaking to Greg]
the preacher.

GREG (now age 43): All those things are true,
and I certainly "ditto" that. I was once on a weekend
retreat with a bunch of men who shared something
of their spiritual journey. As I listened, I was amazed
to realize that of the thirty or so guys I was the only
who could say, "In all of my forty-three years, I have
never known a day without the love of God and the
love of Jesus Christ in my life." Then I thought of
how blessed I was. In our world today that is a pretty
unique statement. My point is, what I had, the other
men didn't. My life was built upon the foundation
of Jesus Christ and the Word of God. When I was
in high school, my mother knew the bad things my
friends did before I knew the bad things they did.
So, why waste the effort of doing bad things, because
I knew my mother was going to find out. My mom
and dad built a spiritual relationship that included
regular church and Sunday School attendance. In
reality, I didn't have a choice.

When we pulled into the church parking lot this morning, I thought back to when we first started coming here. I was about twelve and we didn't even have the Sunday school building next door. When I thought about being in Sunday school each Sunday and having a home life that supported my spiritual foundation, I thank God because it was the greatest gift my parents ever gave me.

BARBARA: Do you remember crying because we missed a couple of Wednesday nights?

GREG: Yeah. Being in the Royal Rangers… talk about having fun within the boundaries… coming to church was fun within the boundaries.

BARBARA: I wonder how many twelve-year-old kids cry because they missed being at church?

GREG: I knew what the right things were because of Christ being in me and because of what my parents taught me. Of course, being a kid you're not always perfect and you do stupid things. But, I also knew it wasn't worth the cost to be rebellious. And I didn't want to disappoint God. Once again I give my parents credit for instilling this mindset in me.

LARRY: My final comment is a word of encouragement to parents and grandparents. As parents God can empower us to do great things. In order to raise kids to be what people have dubbed "spiritual champions," parents need to understand what their values are. Further, parents have, with God's help, a responsibility to communicate those values, even if it goes against the grain of popular culture. And then we need to be authentic in how we live. There was authenticity in our home in the way our parents lived and what they said and did.

As a principle, don't try to fix everything at once. If you are a single parent, ask God to guide you. If you are a couple, ask God to guide you and determine what your priorities are going to be. What do you want to work on first? To the extent that you are open and willing to be guided by Scripture and the Holy Spirit, know God is there to help you. The reality is, as Christians we are not on the home team anymore. We are the "visiting team" in our society. Understand that we can't just lollygag along and get the job done. We've got to really be serious about our godly responsibility as parents and know that God is the one who is going to provide the ability.

BARBARA: We are not perfect, we made mistakes. But God has been faithful and because of our obedience to His Word, God has blessed us over, and over and over. Let me read three verses of Scripture from Ephesians 6:1-3.

Ephesians 6:1: *"Children, obey your parents this is the right thing to do because God has placed them in authority over you."*

Ephesians 6:2: *"Honor your father and mother."* This is the first of God's Ten Commandments that ends with a promise and this promise is Ephesians 6:3: *"If you honor your father and mother, yours will be a long life full of blessings."*

I believe our children need to understand their life will be blessed because of their obedience to their parents. This was one of the verses we gave to Michael when he was in school. And it was a verse we had to give him often until he really understood what it meant.

MICHAEL: I think my back-end remembers that verse pretty well—just kidding!

BARBARA: Does anybody in the audience have any questions they would like to ask?

JOHN HOUNEY (in the audience): I have a two-part question. For the parents here who are raising several children girls and boys; how did you learn the techniques of dealing with each child with such a wide age range and unique personalities? And second, to the boys. How did you guys take these techniques and incorporate them into your own families?

BARBARA: I don't know John. I'm not that smart. It's got to be the grace of God. You who have more than one child know they each have different personalities. All I had to do was to look at Alice and that would be enough correction. With Michael I'd have to discipline him a little more often. I had to learn how each of them felt about certain things and what their needs were.

We always kept the lines of communication open so we could talk to the older children. However with the younger children, especially those under seven years old, I think you need to use the rod as God teaches us in Proverbs. That doesn't mean you use a baseball bat, or a belt or even a wooden spoon. When the Bible talks about "sparing the rod and spoiling the child," it's talking about a switch. It stings like crazy but doesn't leave any lasting effects. It's a little difficult in Arizona because you don't want to use the one with stickers. (One of the boys chimed in: "That cactus really hurt! I'm kidding, I'm kidding."). You can't let a child run you, it just doesn't work.

QUESTION: How did you keep from favoring one child over another?

BARBARA: I don't know. [Posing the question to the boys] Have any of you felt that somebody else was the favorite?

LARRY: I would say we all felt like we were the favorite.

GREG: I would say look at it from the perspective of the amount of time you give each child. If you have three kids and you spend all your time with one kid, the other two will feel neglected. I think it's giving a concentrated focus on each one. Nor do you sit with a stopwatch and time how much time you give to each one.

PERRY: This is an interesting question I have three boys; 25, 24, and 21. The first two are very much alike and it was fairly easy to deal with them. The third one dances to the beat of a different drummer. It's just a fact of life, he's different. It's been difficult to truly know what makes him click. I've repeatedly asked God for wisdom in knowing how best to deal with him in every aspect of life, social as well as spiritual. If you ask for God's wisdom, in prayer, He will be faithful to His promise and give you the wisdom you ask for. I admit I don't do everything right. It doesn't say in the Bible we will. In fact, we're pretty much guaranteed we aren't going to do everything right.

BARBARA: That's why there are so many instructions.

PERRY: Right, I've learned my youngest son is different than the other two, and I, too, don't always do everything right, but I feel in the end, his desire is to serve God, and the expression of his faith will be different than the other two. I've just got to accept the fact that they are not all going to be the same. And, praise God, it would be a pretty boring and weird world if we were all exactly the same. That's why we have this chapter in I Corinthians 13 that talks about love. It's easy to love people who do everything the same way you do. We have to learn to love the ones that maybe are a little bit different.

BARBARA: Love the unlovable. One reason we are sitting around this table [Barbara points to the table placed in the front of the church] is because this is where, at the end of the day, we spent most of our family time together. I know mothers, this is a terrible thing to tell you, but it's important to cook a family a dinner. You need to spend time with your family around the dinner table. With many working moms I know it's not a popular expectation. I'm not real good doing this anymore, but it is possible. When the six kids came to live with us, we had a meal every night. It was a part of our life. It can be done. And dinner was precisely at six o'clock. When my girls left for college it was like, how will I get the potatoes mashed and the gravy made and still have them hot at the same time? I finally learned! That's the reason I chose the table to be put here in front of the church, because the table is an important thing.

DON (in the audience): Was going to church a choice or was it more a standard in your home?

MICHAEL: We had a choice. It was, were we going to ride or walk? (Congregation laughs).

MICHAEL: I totally agree that it was a standard. It wasn't up for discussion. It wasn't Mom waking me up and asking if I wanted to go to church today. You just didn't know any different growing up that you had a choice. It was just what we did every Sunday morning and Wednesday night. And back then it was Sunday nights too. This was just something our household did without discussion. As a parent of three children I've tried to duplicate this same discipline even though there are times it is not always convenient. This is what we do as a family. On Sunday's we go to church.

BARBARA: [Speaking to the boys] When we loaded the car, each had their own place. But one Sunday night we forgot Greg. When we got home he wasn't there and we realized we had left him at church (laughter from congregation).

GREG: I may have been disciplined, but I never felt I wasn't loved. It's always been important for my wife Gina and me that after we spank our child we would love them and explain what was going on. There was always discipline in our growing up years, and there was always love. I never felt unloved because I was disciplined. The Scripture says discipline **is** love, and Hebrews talks about the importance of discipline from God even as adults.

PERRY: For those who are raising younger kids, try to discipline them in a calm manner. This is pretty important. The discipline is for something the child has done wrong wanting their own way, not because I am angry right now. I can remember doing something I was told not to do and Mom walking over to the nearest tree and grabbing a branch and breaking it off. I knew then I was doomed. But she never did it out of anger. It was "you did something wrong because you were disobedient, and we need to take care of it right now." That was a good thing. I was not disciplined just because I made a mistake or didn't do something right. This is something I've tried to do with my kids. I have not been perfect, there have been a few times I've gotten a bit carried away, I disciplined my son as we went **up** the stairs one day because he spent a bunch of money on my credit card without me knowing it. Generally speaking, though, I've remained fairly calm in my discipline.

BARBARA: One of the worst punishments for our kids was not getting to do the fun things

because they hadn't done their chores. The rule was
if you don't do your chores, you don't get to do the
"fun" things. We did a lot of fun things as a family.
They learned that if you didn't want to do the things
necessary to keep the family going, you didn't get
to participate in the "fun" activities either. After a
couple of days of being ostracized by the rest of the
family, they would be ready to do their chores again.

QUESTION (From the audience): When a
child is older (legal age) but still lives at home, at
what point does a mother's input become an invasion of their privacy?

PERRY: I'm 52 and it [instruction from par-
ents] still comes, which I welcome!

BARBARA: As long as they're putting their
feet under your table, you still have the authority.
You make the rules. Use suggestions as the way to
get through to older children. As a mother, you
still have input. That doesn't mean they are going
to follow your suggestions. Michael wasn't supposed to be watching "R" rated movies at college.
He'll tell you that wasn't the best thing for him.
But if a child is still living in your house, still putting their feet under your table, then they should
still live by your rules.

MICHAEL: For the first three summers,
when I came home from college and lived at home,
I said, "I'm going home and I'm older now and
I can do whatever I want with my friends." In
today's culture, such an attitude would be completely normal, except the place I was coming

home to was my parent's house. I knew when I came home it was a matter of courtesy to check in with them. I knew it wasn't right to be a free-for-all those summer months. When I was 22-years-old I still let them know, "Hey, I'm going to be out with my buddies. We're playing basketball. I'll be home at 11:30," It was just a normal right thing to let my parents know what I was doing. I'm staying in their house, sleeping in their bed. If I wanted to go out and get my own apartment and pay the money myself and get a job during school so I could do what I wanted, I would have had their blessing, but that's not what I chose to do. So if I choose to come and live in their house, the rules still apply. I didn't bring my girlfriend over to stay until the late hours of the evening. The rules that were set for me in high school were still the same rules that applied when I was staying at their house.

QUESTION (From the audience): First of all, I commend you for your family concept. How do we talk to kids today faced with contemporary social challenges? How do you tell the kids that things of the world are not the thing to do?

BARBARA: Explain to them why it is not worth it. It is a known fact that the greatest teacher for young people is their parents, even if they don't admit it when they are young. The values they get from your lifestyle and standards will have the greatest influence on them in the long run.

MICHAEL: That's a difficult question. I have probably dealt with issues in my life that

were different from those Perry or Greg had to
deal with. Some of the things I've seen several kids
experience, that they didn't, has probably given me
the ability to see where many of the High School
kids are coming from today. A couple of years ago,
a kid on the football team overdosed on heroin in
his father's house. This was a young man whose
parents had split up and I was trying to help him
through the tough spots in his life. As a coach, I
have observed that kids without an intact family life struggle the most. Almost 90 percent of
the kids who are tempted to get into stuff they
shouldn't, whether it's drugs, alcohol or language,
or whatever the case, come from homes where their
parents have split or divorced or they don't care
what their kids are doing.

One thing we talk about with these kids is
their relationship with their parents. Whether their
parents are single or divorced or whatever, I stress
the importance of showing respect and commitment to them. It is something we are instructed
in Scripture to do. I try to get the kids to understand that regardless of what may have happened
in their life with their parents—and some of these
kids have experienced parental stuff that none of
us would wish on our worst enemy—Jesus Christ
needs to be the center of their life.

These are the things I tell my own children.
I admit that as a dad I'm not perfect, nor is their
mom perfect. Basically, there's only one thing in
this life that is going to be perfect. It is to have

a spiritual foundation centered on Jesus Christ. We're all going to stumble and fall, and the moment you put somebody, even mom or dad on a pedestal, that's where we may get into trouble because that foundation may crumble. Yet, if your foundation is built on Jesus Christ, no matter what direction you go, no matter if it's positive or negative, you've got a solid rock to come back to.

PERRY: One of the things I have discussed with my kids is the question of entitlements. Most young people today feel entitled to have all the answers as well as all of the newest gadgets. They feel entitled to own a car and whatever new fashion comes down the pike. The Bible's answer to entitlements is that none of us is entitled to anything. We're all entitled to hell! That's what we're entitled to, because we're imperfect. Yet our secular society and media have bombarded our young people with the expectation they have the right to have these things. I spend a lot of time dealing with my kids explaining why God gives us rules in the Bible and we have the rules and live the way we do. I explain these rules are not for God's benefit. But God is our Creator and the people that benefit from the principles from God's Word are those who listen and obey the Creator's instructions and rules. They are so we can experience a good, safe and happy life.

For example, when the opportunity is right, I'll sit down and say, "The reason I don't want you out past midnight is because nothing good happens past midnight. I heard that thirty-five, forty

years ago, and it's still true today. You tell me one
thing that absolutely has to be done past midnight.
I don't know of anything. I'll tell you a lot of
things that happen after midnight that aren't good.
I had to be home at midnight. That's just the way
it was. And the times I wasn't home at midnight
were not pleasant, and I understood why.

PASTOR: "Greg thank you: Perry thank
you: Michael thank you: Larry thank you! And
especially to Barbara, thank you on behalf of this
whole church."

FIFTEEN

MY LAST MAJOR CALLING

I have learned the essence of Christianity is to accept the invitation Jesus Christ extends in love, to follow Him and to listen to His words of counsel and direction. Whenever people have in faith made this simple, yet profound choice, their lives take on a new vibrancy, new meaning and a closer commitment to human needs and the work of God's kingdom purposes on earth. What I have also learned is that when God speaks to the inward heart of an individual, and they listen and obey that still small voice, their lives embark on a spiritual adventure far beyond their human imagination.

When my brother Charles first heard a call from God to prepare himself to serve God on the mission field, it took him thirteen years to obey and complete his preparation. When he did, though delayed a few years, he served for the next thirty years with remarkable distinction as a cross-cultural medical missionary in Kenya. Those of you who have read this far know that over the past forty years there have been several occasions when the Lord has given Barbara and me a special word of instruction. The most telling, of course, was in 1969 when contrary to all human reasoning God spoke to my heart and told me to "build a new house on the land you recently bought and take these six orphaned children to raise." The voice in my mind and heart was so clear I knew it was a direct word from the Lord.

To be sure, some of the words we believe came from God haven't been as significant as others. But every time we heard this still small voice speak to our hearts, and we obeyed, our lives were often dramatically changed for a lifetime. My main reason for writing this book is to bear witness to the faithfulness of our Lord in every detail of our lives. As I conclude this book I want to share the last word I received from the Lord. It came in the summer of 2005. I believed this word to be so important it has absorbed much of my time ever since.

That summer my brother Charles and his wife Marlene, along with Barbara and I, attended a David Wilkerson conference held at Radio Music Hall in New York City. For many who attended the conference the anointing of the Lord was a powerful presence. Curiously, the word spoken wasn't at all related to the theme of the conference. Rather, it happened while I was in my hotel room and what I heard was simply, "Campaign Save America." When I asked the Lord for a fuller meaning and understanding of this word, I was convicted to start a campaign to save the core values of "Christian America." It's also interesting that six years later I still do not know its full meaning. Did it mean if America's deteriorating social norms didn't change, God's judgment was imminent? I can't really say.

I do know since 1971, when the Lord revealed the identity of the "beast" prophesied in Revelation chapter thirteen to Charles and then to me, I have spent thousands of hours in research and study to confirm the truth of this revelation. This has given me an understanding of how this will affect the body of Christ in America. Because of my love for America, I am greatly concerned about the tremendous spiritual warfare perpetrated by our enemy to destroy the spiritual heritage and influence of Christianity in our country.

I also know it's not only God's desire for all people to secure salvation in His name, it is also God's will for his people to be involved in the human situation, as was Christ himself, to preserve all that is good in humanity. This is obvious by the great extremes God went to, to save and warn Israel as a nation before He disciplined them. I believe Christians are to function as the salt of the earth, in order to preserve the good. I know too that our only hope to save what was called "Christian America" is for Christians to do all they can to restore the Christian values the majority of Americans lived by, until recent years, since the founding of our nation. To accomplish this, my call from the Lord in these last days is to do all I can to equip Christians to be well grounded in the important principles from His Word.

My **first** leading in this campaign was to write a new book that summarized the topics the Lord had taught me through forty years of research and study. The book *Salt & Light, Fulfilling God's Mission for America In These Last Days* was published in 2007. The book has also been revised into a thirteen-week Bible study, now titled; *You Are Salt & Light, Equipping Christians For These Last Days.*

This book presents the core message of what the Lord taught Barbara and me in guiding our family and my Campaign to Save Christian values in America. It gives the reader a viewpoint from the Word of God so they can understand the prophetic Scriptures and the Christian's walk as it relates to the spiritual warfare now taking place in America. I believe it is critical for Christians to equip themselves and to put on the full armor of God (Ephesians 6:10-18) if they are to successfully withstand the enemy's escalated attacks against the body of Christ and the American family in these last days.

My **second** leading in this campaign was to write a thirty-two page booklet titled, *Campaign Save Christian America*[1]. Some of the topics include: Why America is in danger; a brief history of the six major interventions from God in America's spiritual development; an important spiritual truth about Satan and the tactics he is using to attack America; how our fruit reveals spiritual deception, and the effects of the current spiritual warfare on the body of Christ. There is a corrective action plan that I have been developing that will work to thwart the enemy and I believe could be used to help usher in the next Great Awakening. The details of what has been developed and how you can participate are shared in the balance of this and the next chapter.

My **third** major leading in this campaign has been to work with one of our country's spiritual leaders to develop a teaching series for pastors and Bible teachers based on my book, "*Salt & Light*." He is Dr. David Mains. For over three decades, ministers have looked to Dr. Mains as their friend. Many consider him to be a master teacher of effective preaching. Over the years, he has been a master teacher helping men and women to become life-changing speakers. His background includes a decade as senior pastor of Circle Church in Chicago. For twenty years he directed the "Chapel of the Air," a radio and TV program that won him the 1995 National Religious Broadcasters Programmer of the Year award. He conceptualized and wrote the "50 Day Spiritual

---

1. Approximately 200,000 copies of this booklet have already been distributed to Christians throughout America. We supply them at no charge, asking only that the person ordering the booklet send $.40 each with a minimum order of 10 to cover our postage and handling. For orders of 25 copies or more, our postage and handling is reduced per copy to $.30 each.

Adventure" series used by pastors and lay leaders in over 50,000 churches with more than 5 million participants. Dr. Mains has authored over twenty books, including winning a Gold Medallion Award.

This is what Dr. Mains wrote in an open letter about our working together and my book, *Salt & Light*:

> "*Have you ever read a book that really challenged your preconceptions and changed the way you think? It happened to me not long ago.*
>
> *My son sent me **Salt and Light** by Bob Fraley, a book he had read and asked me for my opinion on its teaching. I didn't know anything about the author, but I'm always in the market for an interesting book.*
>
> *A few days later, I was at home reading the book at my desk when I reached a point where I had to put the book down. The ideas were so startling and so revolutionary that I got up and started pacing back and forth while I considered what I had just read. I quickly understood that if what Bob Fraley was saying in his book **Salt and Light** was true, it had profound implications for the Church today. More than that, I realized it had profound implications for my own life. I sat down and read the rest of the book all the way through!*
>
> *When I finished, I felt like someone had grabbed my backbone through my stomach and shaken me around a bit. It was a message I personally needed to hear, and I believe it's a message that every Believer needs to hear as well. Of course, you don't need me to tell you how popular prophecy is right now. People*

want to know what's coming next. But we need to ask this question: Is most of what people are being taught about prophecy current with what we now know?

*After reading **Salt and Light,** I wanted to meet the author. So I flew from my home in Chicago to Phoenix and had dinner with Bob Fraley and his wife Barbara. I got to know him as a person and learned he has an incredible life story. Let me share just a small portion of that story.*

The Fraley's now have 65 in their family including children, spouses, grandchildren and great-grandchildren, everyone, except those too young, serve the Lord. Their family has not experienced any of the contemporary problems, like drug issues, alcohol challenges or rebellion against family values even though most all of their family members have been active in school, the community and business. How has the Fraley family been so successful during these severe times that have seen biblical values in America deteriorate more in this last generation than in all of the previous years of our country's history?

In June of 1971, Bob went through what I describe as a revolutionary encounter with the Lord. In a word, the Lord opened his spiritual eyes to see the intense warfare the enemy would be waging against Christian values in America during this period of time we are now living that Scripture calls the Last Days. He and his wife Barbara believed the Lord. Of course we can now look back and see that what they were shown has happened over the last 40 years.

Opening his eyes to this conflict for the hearts and

*minds of the American people became the foundation
the Lord used to guide Bob and Barbara in raising
godly children in an increasingly godless society.*

*Soon after his encounter with the Lord in 1971,
God placed a message in his heart that was so strong
and important that it couldn't be ignored. Bob was
inspired to spend hundreds and hundreds of hours
studying the prophetic Scriptures about the Last Days,
especially what he was shown about America's role
and the Christian walk. It's during these times that
our spiritual enemy is so successful in attacking the
lives of Christians and their families as the enemy
attempts to destroy Christian America.*

*The biblical principles the Lord taught the
Fraley's has equipped them for living victoriously during these times of heavy spiritual warfare in America.
Bob shares these Scriptural principles in his book **Salt
and Light**. From his message you can learn how to
equip yourself and your family to counter the enemy's
destructive plans. It will help provide spiritual safety
for your family, our churches and our nation in this
time of great peril.*

*What I discovered about Bob and Barbara, their
family and all his study gave me a feel for the credibil-
ity of his faith and desire to know what the Bible actually says. I was so moved by what I read in his book I
decided to do something I hadn't done in years. Based
on Bob's book I wrote a new **50 Day Spiritual
Adventure** called **The Remarkable Revelation**.*

*I sense how important it is to help Bob Fraley
with his mission of equipping Christians for these*

Last Days. Satan has been successful at destroying the spiritual foundations on which our country was built and we are reaping the consequences. Many spiritual leaders agree that we are living in the Last Days, therefore, they are saying that it is possible we haven't seen anything yet!

Just as the Lord told Noah to build a physical ark to protect his family from the flood, we must prepare our "spiritual arks" so that we can be equipped along with our children and grandchildren to survive the flood of spiritual attacks that are sweeping our nation and are going to get worse. Considerable expense has gone into an effort to help equip you for these Last Days. Bob Fraley's Christian organization Christian Life Outreach has provided funds to send you a **free copy** of his book **Salt and Light**, which is a full size 6' X 9" book with over 200 pages with many copies sold at full retail price of $14.95.

Tommy Barnett, Pastor of Phoenix First Assembly of God, one of the largest churches in America and founder of the Dream Center states: "This book carries a powerful message. I truly believe God will use it to spark a new awakening in the church. I thoroughly recommend it."

Larry Neville, President of Praise Chapel Fellowship denomination says: "If I were to write a book, this book says everything that I would want to say. I support Bob in every way I can to get his message out."

Sending for your **free copy** of **Salt & Light** and the other free items Christian Life Outreach will send you is a great way for you, your pastor or Bible

*teacher to get a look at this powerful new Spiritual
Adventure series Bob and I developed and his book.
You will see how they can make an enormous positive
impact to help equip you, and your church or Bible
study group for these last days.*

*The prophecies of the Word of God are unfolding
before our eyes. America is moving quickly away from
being a Christian nation. It is unquestionable that
our spiritual foundations are under spiritual attack.
Yet far too many people are oblivious to the cause and
danger that lies ahead.*

*I see the American Church like a family in a
home that's on fire but they don't yet know it and they
need someone to cry out "Wake Up-Danger!" They
need to have something or someone there who will
help guide and equip them for what's ahead. This
is what the message of Bob Fraley's book will do. I
needed this message and so does each Christian. I urge
you to send for this free book and information on our
new series,* **The Remarkable Revelation: 50 Days
to Prepare for What's Ahead** *for yourself, your
pastor and others so they can evaluate this critical
message for these Last Days! There is no limit on how
many* **free books** *you request.*

*Though Christian Life Outreach will send you
Bob's book free of charge they do have a cost of about
$6.00 for postage and handling and need for you to
help with this cost. They thank you for helping them
in this way! (See the back of this book for the details if
you want to get your free copy of* **Salt & Light**.)*

For His Church, Dr. David Mains

*P.S. We do not want to make the same mistake the Jewish Nation made when Christ came the first time. They did not understand the prophetic Scriptures about their day; therefore, were not prepared and totally missed the incarnation, when God became man and visited planet Earth. God has given us key prophetic Scriptures to help equip Christians for our day. Bob Fraley's message in his book **Salt & Light** is the best thing I have seen to equip Christians for what's ahead. The spiritual battles and deception of the enemy will cause many in our churches great suffering unless we help them. I know that Bob's book will challenge your thinking and give you a new perspective on Revelation, especially the key chapter—Chapter 13, which identifies the beast. We're looking forward to sharing this powerful message with you.*

The **fourth** leading I received relating to this Campaign to Save Christian America and equipping Christians to build their spiritual ark for these last days was to write another 32-page booklet titled, *A Time For Action: How to Spiritually Prepare For What's Ahead.* Similar to the *Campaign Save Christian America* booklet thousands have already been distributed throughout America. It too is available at no charge for just the cost of handling and postage.

At the back of this book you will find the details for receiving your **free copy** of *Salt & Light* along with other free materials that include a DVD of an interview with Dr. Mains and me and both of the **32 page booklets**. *Christian Life Outreach* is only asking that you help by sending them their postage cost and packing expense of $6.00 for each copy of **Salt & Light**. There is no limit as to the number you may order so you can share this book with your pastor, relatives and friends.

SIXTEEN

BUILDING YOUR FAMILY'S
SPIRITUAL ARK

Jesus said: *"Just as it was in the days of Noah, so also will it be in the days of the Son of Man* [referring to the time of His return]. *People were eating, drinking, marrying and being given in marriage up to the day Noah entered the ark. Then the flood came and destroyed them all. It was the same in the days of Lot. People were eating and drinking, buying and selling, planting and building. But the day Lot left Sodom, fire and sulfur rained down from heaven and destroyed them all. It will be just like this on the day the Son of Man is revealed"* (Luke 17:26-30).

If we are living in a day similar to that of Noah, it would be wise for us to look at how he prepared for his last days as we prepare for ours. The Bible says, *"By faith Noah, when warned about things not yet seen, in holy fear built an ark to save his family"* (Hebrews 11:7).

This verse exemplifies Barbara's and my walk with the Lord that for over 40 years has been with a heart of obedience and holy fear. I have shared our testimony as an encouragement to help others see God's love and faithfulness. The question now becomes, "Why should I consider building an ark?" and, "How, in these days of heavy spiritual warfare, can I be better equipped to build a spiritual ark that will protect and save my family?"

Momentum is a highly-valued concept for success in almost every aspect of life. In the world of sports, it's to be on a roll. A team functioning in sync with high momentum appears almost unstoppable. Championships are won or lost depending on which team captures the momentum. The world of politics is also similar. Candidates for office want their campaigns to peak at just the right time. It's important for a wave of momentum to mark their efforts just before people vote.

In Ken Burns' captivating 15-hour documentary series about World War II, we're reminded, at the start of that global conflict; the Axis powers had all the momentum on their side. In Europe, the Nazi blitzkrieg had proven unstoppable. The same was true of Japan's lightning strikes in the Far East. If General Tojo had chosen to penetrate Southeast Asia, instead of attacking America's naval base in Hawaii, he probably would have captured the resources he desired without provoking America to war. And, if Hitler had completed the conquest of England before turning his troops on Russia, the outcome in that theater of conflict would no doubt have been markedly different. It was these ill-conceived decisions that had a negative effect on the momentum their troops had previously enjoyed.

In spiritual warfare, it's also vital for the Christian Church to have the high ground of momentum. Alas, according to Dave Olson in his book *The American Church in Crisis*, "The Church in America [has lost its momentum] is not booming."[1] All but those who haven't a clue as to what's going on would say that in America it's Satan who in the past several decades has captured the momentum.

---

1. Dave T. Olson, *The American Church in Crisis* (Grand Rapids: Zondervan 2008), pp. 16, 185.

It's not that the church in the U.S. is impotent. It's just that it doesn't have anywhere near the societal clout it once did.

I believe the 21st Century committed follower of Jesus Christ faces some of the greatest challenges ever in the history of the Church as the devil has never had a greater opportunity to tempt people as easily as he does now. No longer does he have to lure us to some dimly lit part of town to show us his wares. He boldly comes right into our homes via the Internet, DVDs, TV, radio, CDs, magazines, books, you name it. His evil enticements are made conveniently available, and all too many Christians find his offerings attractive. They expose themselves to the principle where they are tempted above that which they can handle. Our country's Christian heritage continues to take hit after hit as though there is an unstated national effort to distance ourselves from our Christian past. The new emphasis is on tolerance that mocks the term "Christian America" as outdated, embarrassing, and even offensive.

Since 1971, when the Lord inspired me to explore His Word about the end-times, I discovered nothing in my research that would diminish the prophetic truth in Scripture, and nothing in whom we are as a people, that prohibits the U.S. from becoming a backslidden Christian nation. Nor is there a probation period given to the U.S. by the Lord as the majority of people have forgotten our country's founding Christian principles and values, which of course, is Satan's goal. Many Americans now treat the sacred with an attitude of contempt. They dismiss Christianity as more or less irrelevant for moderns. It's a secular mindset that sets aside spiritual contributions as being mostly meaningless and goes beyond ignoring the church to ridiculing and debasing it.

Scripture is clear. When the Jewish nation obeyed God's laws they experienced firsthand God's presence and witnessed His miracles and blessings. When they were in rebellion or ignored

His laws, they were vulnerable to Satan's deception. For example, Israel totally missed the incarnation. When God became man and visited planet Earth the Bible says, *Jesus came unto His own and His own received Him not*. Has Satan, masquerading as an angel of light, once again used deception to fool a nation, as he did the Jews at the time of the first coming of Jesus?

<u>Deception always breeds compromise, which brings about spiritual defeat</u>. Satan has tricked many Christians into accepting the secular world's philosophy of life, which has opened the door for him to oppress and browbeat Christians with varying degrees of brokenness, confusion and psychological distress. Sunday after Sunday, broken wounded people fill our church pews. Families are falling apart as divorce among Christians almost equals that of the secular world; young people are doing themselves in; church leaders are giving up.

Our Western humanistic culture (prodded by Satan, the father of lies) has too often manipulated and duped people into believing their self-centered pursuit of wealth and security is rooted in this passing world. Unhappily Christians are not immune from this deception. A few years ago Dr. Billy Graham stated that according to his research, a high percentage of American Christians are living spiritually defeated lives.

Through its ceaseless search for materialistic prosperity, our Western society has created a climate that makes it difficult to celebrate the supernatural or spiritual dimensions of life. As a result, the Christian message is silenced and celebrations of historical facts like Christmas and Easter are increasingly banned from the public square because they are deemed to be too religious. Government legislation has enacted laws never contemplated by an earlier generation. Such laws actually work against our historic standards that include the way we raise our families, run our schools, and set ethics and moral values in business and government. The most obvious example is the law that allows for an abortion on demand. This hideous law has allowed the killing of more than 50 million innocent babies.

Since World War II, the divorce rate has skyrocketed, and the Church hasn't been spared. Greed and unethical conduct has tainted such professionals as doctors, politicians, ministers, corporate executives, educators, lawyers, athletes and other pillars of society. Large areas of our great cities have been turned into stalking grounds for gang violence, sexual perversions, crime and drug-dealing. We now have the largest prison population in the world. Our rate of incarceration is more than seven times higher than that of most other nations. Addiction to pornography has reached epidemic levels for both Christians and non-Christians. Our country, which once had such a strong Christian foundation, has experienced an overwhelming increase in lawlessness, permissiveness, rebellion and selfishness. The percentage of young adults who adhere to biblically based values has, since WW II, dropped from 65% to 4%.

Is it too much to claim that the standards in our country have deteriorated more in this last generation than in all the previous ones since our forefathers founded America? For these and other reasons, committed followers of Jesus often find it difficult to maintain a faithful witness. In order for Christians to be victorious in their spiritual battle, they need to be to be equipped with the weapons and armor of Ephesians 6:10-18 (NIV).

> "Finally, be strong in the Lord and in his mighty
> power. Put on the full armor of God so that you can
> take your stand against the devil's schemes. For our
> struggle is not against flesh and blood, but against

*the rulers, against the authorities, against the powers
of this dark world and against the spiritual forces of
evil in the heavenly realms. Therefore put on the full
armor of God, so that when the day of evil comes* [it
has arrived!]*, you may be able to stand your ground,
and after you have done everything, to stand. Stand
firm then, with the belt of truth buckled around your
waist, with the breastplate of righteousness in place,
and with your feet fitted with the readiness that comes
from the gospel of peace. In addition to all this, take
up the shield of faith, with which you can extinguish
all the flaming arrows of the evil one. Take the helmet
of salvation and the sword of the Spirit, which is the
word of God. And pray in the Spirit on all occasions
with all kinds of prayers and requests."*

I believe it is because our country has been at the center of
Christian teaching and activity during the last century that it has
become the special focus of Satan's deceptive warfare. His strategy, as presented in prophetic Scriptures, reveals he has reserved
his fiercest onslaughts for these last days. He has systematically
attacked and removed as many biblical standards in our country
as he can, and then moved in to pillage and destroy. If we are to
prevent him from continuing to tear down our families and our
nation, we must rethink our strategy of resistance.

Unfamiliarity with the biblical principles of spiritual warfare
has left many Christians idle while Satan wages war with terrify-
ing success in these last days. People in the secular culture know
the importance of understanding a competitor's tactics. Whether
in business, sports, military operations or even video games, people carefully prepare themselves for defense and counterattack.

But how many in the family of God know about the tactics of our enemy in the end-times? Many Christians live defeated lives because they don't see Satan and his worldly agenda as the root cause of their problems; therefore, they have not prepared for the warfare taking place in our country. Their worlds continue to fall apart, and these troubled individuals don't know why. Many pastors, and scores of professional counselors, expend much of their energies caring for broken and soul-damaged Christians.

In the Old Testament we have an example of how Satan's tactics worked in Egypt. Pharaoh fooled the Israelites into serving Him. Exodus 1:11 states that the Egyptians *"put slave masters over them* [the Israelites] *to oppress them with forced labor, and they built Pithom and Rameses as store cities for Pharaoh."* That is one of the saddest truths found in the Bible. Rather than the Israelites using their numerical strength and the power of the Lord to wrest free of Pharaoh's grasp, Satan exploited their ignorance to make his regime stronger. The Israelites contributed to their own oppression, and Pharaoh tightened the screws. Exodus 1:14 states that he *"made their lives bitter with hard labor in brick and mortar with all kinds of work in the fields; in all their hard labor the Egyptians used them ruthlessly."* Just as Pharaoh burdened the Israelites, Satan is now oppressing Christians with the ways of the world. The lesson God has given us from the history of Israel is that we do not have to remain in bondage. Through the cross of Christ, Satan is a defeated enemy.

Only by God's grace and mercy did Barbara and I become equipped to build a spiritual ark for our family. The key was discovering the shocking revelation that revealed the identity of the "beast/superpower" in Revelation 13. It opened our spiritual eyes to see the tremendous spiritual warfare the enemy would wage against Christian values in America. I believe Satan is on the warpath to destroy Christian America. Understanding this placed a holy fear within our hearts that became the foundation for our obedience to the Word of God and His guidance in building our spiritual ark.

From the experience of what the Lord has taught Barbara and me over the last 40 years, we want to <u>help you build your "spiritual ark" of safety for your family in these last days</u>. The spiritual principles the Lord taught us have stood the test of time, even when our country's moral values have deteriorated so drastically, and they will help you live in safety despite the enemy's brutal attacks. Every Christian needs to build their own spiritual ark and the Lord may direct you differently than He did us. The needs of every family and their purpose in serving the Lord are somewhat different. However, the spiritual principles taught in God's Word will be the same. The Lord will bless those who walk before Him in "holy fear" with a heart of obedience. The key for spiritual victory has never changed.

We are involved in a severe warfare for the hearts and minds of the people in our nation. As more believers become involved, the fury of this battle will intensify. The enemy will not let up, he knows his time is short and will fight hard to deceive and weaken the Church with jealousies, greed, indifference and the list of Galatians 5:19-21. This means we need to understand God's Word and what it has to say about how the devil conducts his end-times warfare. It also means our being equipped with the weapons of spiritual warfare so we can stave off his attacks and prevent loved ones from being ravaged.

Over the last few years I have put considerable effort, time and expense into preparing materials that will help equip Christians to understand this spiritual warfare taking place in America. The materials I have developed will teach you <u>how</u> to build your spiritual ark for the saving of your family in these last days.

I suspect many would conclude such an undertaking as trying to call Christian America back to biblical values and to help save the Christian family is too huge a task for one or two people. And though there are other organizations who desire a spiritual reformation of American Christianity, I believe my message—focused on equipping Christians for these last days—is unique.

After Dr. Mains and I met, our interaction led to a new and exciting level of cooperation between our ministries. Some of our thinking resulted in a new Scriptural perspective that included *The Fifty Day Spiritual Adventure* series and several of my other publications. David Mains and I believe God has planned and prepared this new *Spiritual Adventure* series for His Church. During these days of uncertainty, I believe biblical prophecy is worthy of serious and thoughtful study. While many people who are interested in this subject get their ideas and information from pop culture and fiction, my emphasis is on the Bible.

The *Spiritual Adventure* Dr. Mains and I have developed along with my book *Salt & Light* will help believers interpret current events and the future in light of Scripture. It will also challenge and equip the body of Christ with the spiritual building materials to construct their own "spiritual ark." This powerful series along with my book, *Salt & Light* will probe for answers to such questions as:

- What does the Bible say about America in these last days?
- What is the great superpower discussed in Revelation 13?
- What will happen to the Church?

This study explores a variety of Scriptures including the prototype of all the prophetic writings in Scripture, found in the book of Daniel. The themes of the Old Testament, with its concern for specific men and women with names and families, and personal histories of people like Abraham, Isaac, Jacob, Ruth,

Esther and Rahab is surprisingly up-to-date. Thus, no matter what Christians face today, similar or parallel issues are found in the Old Testament, i.e., those who were in rebellion against God and those who chose to live a life of obedience, to Him.

A key for our spiritual preparedness for what's ahead is to participate in the new *50-Day Spiritual Adventure,* **The Remarkable Revelation: 50 Days to Prepare for What's Ahead**. This powerful preaching series for your church will make the prophecies of Scripture come alive in new ways. It emphasizes spiritual truths combined with specific action steps that will prepare you for both the present and the future. Prophecy is one of the most important topics in the Bible for "ark-builders." This powerful series will not only challenge you individually, but rally the church to be what God expects of it in this critical time.

Some of the topics included in this series are:

- Guidelines for understanding prophetic writings.
- How to recognize the enemy's deceptive ways.
- Preparing for the possibility of religious persecution.
- Protecting your children and grandchildren in a wicked world.
- Why we need revival in church—and how to get it.
- How to experience the joy of personal revival.
- Discovering the urgency of "Hosanna," which means "Save us NOW!"
- Watching for the coming King.

We have prepared written messages for each one of these topics, along with more than 600 high resolution Power Point graphics to be used by whoever is teaching this series. There are also 14 videos professionally produced in high resolution projection quality files to introduce each message. In addition, Dr.

Mains has written an Adult Bible-Study Journal with questions for each of the 50 days so you can see in your own handwriting how God has aided your progress, and for this Adventure, I have also written a short paperback book titled *The Day That Changed America*.

Pastors have used this powerful *50 Day Spiritual Adventure* format to lead their congregations to new levels of spiritual growth and development. Lay leaders have used it for Sunday school classes, Bible studies and accountability groups and have given it to their pastors and church leaders as a gift to their entire church—or used it for their own families.

REV. REYES TORRES from New York used "The Remarkable Revelation: 50 Days to Prepare for What's Ahead" in his church and wrote: *"The sessions have been very interactive and have encouraged the attendees to build an ark for their families; we are seeing that effectively being lived out. I was asked by my District Superintendent to do a ... seminar based on the material ... for the pastors of our district."*

HAROLD SHARP of Pennsylvania told us: *"The study provided an excellent scriptural understanding to what is happening in our day and* [gave us] *the way to prepare ourselves, families, and churches, spiritually for the days ahead."*

CHAPLAIN CLEM ROGGENBACK of California did the study with his wife. He wrote: *"This was one of my favorite Bible Studies—very professionally put together to make it enjoyable to look up the answers. The questions causing one to make commitments were good. My wife ... had fun doing it with me."*

WHAT OTHERS HAVE SAID ABOUT PREVIOUS 50-DAY ADVENTURE SERIES

"I have observed the tremendous effect and blessing the 50-Day Spiritual Adventures has on a church fellowship. I unreservedly and heartily

recommend the Adventures for any congregation and pastor." CLIFF BAR-
ROWS, MUSIC/PROGRAM DIRECTOR, BILLY GRAHAM CRUSADES

"The creative 50-Day Spiritual Adventures are as soundly based
in God's Word as they are fruitful in advancing God's Spirit! Team
up!" PASTOR JACK W. HAYFORD.

"God has used the 50-Day Spiritual Adventures to touch the
lives of millions of people around the world. ... I strongly recommend
the 50-Day Spiritual Adventure as a life-changing experience."
JOE ALDRICH, PRESIDENT MULTNOMAH BIBLE COLLEGE & NORTH-
WEST PRAYER RENEWAL.

"At a time when our nation is in need of a genuine spiritual
awakening to Christ, the 50-Day Spiritual Adventure has proven
to be a superb tool to help everyday Christians step boldly into the
streams of revival. It is a pastor's dream come true." DAVID BRYANT,
PRESIDENT CONCERTS OF PRAYER INTERNATIONAL.

"I wish you could read even a fraction of the thousands and thousands of letters that have come across my desk telling about the value
of the 50-Day Spiritual Adventure. You would immediately make
up your mind to get involved, and your only question would be why
you hadn't done this sooner." DAVID R. MAINS, DIRECTOR MAINSTAY
MINISTRIES, IL

"Many people want to grow spiritually but need something to
give them a boost. The 50-Day Spiritual Adventure will do it."
STUART BRISCOE, PASTOR, WI

I invite you to visit our web site to see the other tools we have
developed to help the Christian community live in victory during
these prophetic days: www.bobfraleychristianlifeoutreach.com.

The materials are designed to prepare you spiritually as you
do battle against our enemy and the collapsing foundations of our
nation. To see the tide turn will require the individual commitment by millions of American Christians.

"You are the salt of the earth. But if the salt loses its saltiness, how can it be made salty again? It is no longer good for anything, except to be thrown out and trampled by men. You are the light of the world. A city on a hill cannot be hidden. Neither do people light a lamp and put it under a bowl. Instead they put it on its stand, and it gives light to everyone in the house. In the same way, let your light shine before men, that they may see your good deeds and praise your Father in heaven" (Matthew 5:13-14 (NIV).

There have never been more penetrating words spoken to Christians than these words spoken by Jesus. It is the <u>mission statement</u> for every follower of Christ.

There is an order form on the back page of this book so you can begin your preparation now by ordering your free copy of the book *Salt & Light.* Or, you can call in your order by phoning 1-866-998-4136. You can also go online to order the book at www.bobfraley christianlifeoutreach.com. Click on (order online).

I do not take any revenue received from the sale of the books I have written, from speaking engagements, or the *50 Day Spiritual Adventure* series. Monies received are used for the cost of operating *Christian Life Outreach,* a non-profit organization, and for helping our missionary outreach in Africa, and our ministry through our Christian retreat center. You can learn more about all of these projects through our web site, www.bobfraleychristianlifeoutreach.com.

I do ask that when you send for your free copy of my book, *Salt & Light* that you help *Christian Life Outreach* by sending $6.00 for each copy to cover their postage and handling expense.

My final request is to encourage you to help lead, with some of your Christian friends, an effort to purchase this *Remarkable*

Revelation Spiritual Adventure for your church or Bible-study group. Originally this package sold for $149.95, but we have been able to lower the cost to $99.95, which is extremely reasonable considering the costs involved in developing the many professionally produced items supplied to teach or preach this unique 8-10 week Series.

If you are interested in helping to save Christian America and for Christians to build their "spiritual ark" for the saving of their families in these last days, we have the materials to assist you. We suggest you start by sharing this book, *The Blessings of Obedience* and *Salt & Light* with relatives, friends, pastors and people of spiritual influence in their surrounding areas.

Another area of opportunity for those who are willing to participate in the "Campaign to Save Christian America" and "Help Save the Christian Family" would be to conduct a Bible class or try to find a Bible teacher that would conduct a class either in your church or community using the book *You Are Salt & Light: Equipping Christians for These Last Days*. This is the revised and published 13-week Bible study edition of *Salt & Light* with discussion questions at the end of each chapter.

If you have an interest in the possibility of joining with other spiritual warriors to save Christian America, we would like to hear from you. To let us know you can use the reply form in the back of this book or contact us through e-mail, xnlifeout@ yahoo.com. To find out more about my ministry visit my web site, www.bobfraleychristianlifeoutreach.com. You may also follow our ministries via Twitter, Facebook, and my blog; accessed through the same web site.

Send for your **free copy** of my book *Salt & Light* today. Along with each free book *Christian Life Outreach* will also send you a free starter pack for our new *Spiritual Adventure* teaching series titled, *The Remarkable Revelation: 50 Days to Prepare for What's Ahead*. Each starter pack has:

- A DVD of a half-hour television program with David Mains and me. This interview reviews the new *50-Day Spiritual Adventure*.
- Week one sample sermon.
- Complete series outline matrix.
- A promotional flyer.
- A copy of both 32 page booklets, *A Time For Action* and *Campaign Save Christian America*.

To help equip families for these last days, in addition to the above items, *Christian Life Outreach* will also send you as many copies of this testimony book, *The Blessings of Obedience* to share with relatives and friends—retail value of $9.95 each—for only $3.00 each, their cost of handling and postage, if you order a minimum of five or more copies. If you just want to order one copy of this book the handling and postage cost will be $5.00 each. You can also order, *Salt & Light* and the *Blessings of Obedience* together. The postage and handling cost will only be $8.00 for both books if they can be mailed at the same time to one location.

I close this book with a prayer that the body of Christ will have a new understanding of the materials needed to build their own spiritual ark. My prayer for the Church is also Paul's prayer from Colossians 1:11-14 (NLT).

> *We also pray that you will be strengthened with all*
> *his glorious power so you will have the endurance and*
> *patience you need. May you be filled with joy, always*
> *thanking the Father. He has enabled you to share in*

the inheritance that belong to his people who live in the light. For he has rescued us from the kingdom of darkness and transferred us into the kingdom of his dear Son, who purchased our freedom and forgave our sins.

EPILOGUE

It is fall of 2010 and the manuscript for this book is finished and being typeset. After finishing this book the Lord led me to do something that I never thought would happen. It was difficult for me to understand and obey.

You read in chapter thirteen how the Lord guided and blessed the development of my manufacturing company, ALEXCO. Through the years ALEXCO has grown to be a very successful supplier of one of the most difficult aluminum products to produce; the product is used in fabricating the fuselage, wings and tail sections of airplanes. There are only two other major producers in the U.S. that meet the quality demands required in supplying this product; therefore, have been certified by the aerospace industry.

About three years ago Kaiser Aluminum, a major corporation that also supplies aluminum products to the aerospace industry (but does not produce the aluminum product we produce), approached me to buy ALEXCO. They made what seemed to be a fair offer; however, I declined and let them know ALEXCO was not for sale. ALEXCO has been an excellent family business. All three of our sons work for the company. I have remained as Chairman and CEO and appointed Perry, our oldest son, President, Greg, our middle son, Vice President of Business Affairs and Michael, our youngest son Vice President of Marketing and

Sales. All three have been excellent leaders and contributors to the success of the company.

During the last three years Kaiser continued to pursue us to sell them ALEXCO. Their owning ALEXCO would complete their manufacturing position of producing all of the raw aluminum products used in the aerospace industry. Airplane producers are seeking more and more to sign contracts with those raw material manufacturers that can supply all of the aluminum products they require.

This last summer John Barneson, Kaiser's Vice President of Development, called to ask if I would meet with Jack Hockema, their President, CEO and Chairman of the board. As I discussed ALEXCO's position with Jack, I said I might consider selling forty percent because of the advantage for both companies to be in a position to supply all of the raw aluminum products used in the aerospace industry.

We were close to an agreement for a forty percent purchase when their anti-trust attorney advised Kaiser that the only way they could be sure of avoiding any anti-trust problems would be for them to be the exclusive sales agent. This meant my son Michael and his entire sales force would have to go to work for Kaiser. I knew this would never fly with Michael or anyone else at ALEXCO as it would open the door for ALEXCO to lose all of the excellent customer relationships we had developed over the last thirteen years. I tabled the possibility of a forty percent sale.

Our oldest son Perry then came to me with a different thought. He said, "Dad, Kaiser has been pursuing us to buy the company for three years and just won't go away. Could this be something that is of the Lord?" That was an interesting and challenging thought. The way Kaiser continued to call us over the last three years reminded us of a story we once heard. The story is about a man who was warned of a terrible flood that was coming. As the

rain came and had flooded the first floor of his house a boat came
to pick him up and the man responded by saying, "I am not wor-
ried, the Lord will take care of me." The rains continued to pour
down and as he had now retreated to the second story of his house
another boat came to pick him up and he again refused to get into
the boat responding, "The Lord will take care of me." As the water
continued to rise and he had to go up to the roof of his house, a
helicopter came to pick him up and yet again he stated, "The Lord
will take care of me." The water soon covered the entire house and
the man drowned. Upon entering heaven he asked the Lord why
He had not taken care of him and had let him drown. The Lord
replied, "Three times I sent someone to pick you up—twice by
boat and once by a helicopter—and three times you refused."

Though this is just a story, the thought it conveys did help
us to consider that perhaps Kaiser's persistence in wanting to buy
ALEXCO was something being orchestrated by the Lord. If our
selling to Kaiser was of the Lord, I certainly did not want to "miss"
His direction. Therefore, to put our question before the Lord about
selling the company, Perry suggested that we use the biblical principle (as Gideon did in Judges 6:36-40) of putting a *fleece* before
the Lord that would seem impossible for man to fulfill. Our three
sons, Barbara and I, who make up ALEXCO's board, all agreed.
So we put a *fleece* before the Lord and the *fleece* was based on our
selling one hundred percent of the company.

I advised John Barneson, Kaiser's Senior Vice President of
our *fleece*. He is a Christian so I knew he would understand
the meaning of using a *fleece* to receive the Lord's direction. He
said, "Bob that would be impossible." However, in a few days
their president called from his office in Los Angeles and spoke
with my son Perry. Barbara and I were at our farm in Ohio. He
said, "Perry, I want to lease a business jet and stop in Phoenix to

pick-up you, Greg and Michael, and fly back to the farm to meet with your Dad."

We met with Kaiser's President and to my surprise the Lord answered the *fleece*! That was a difficult leading and somewhat heartbreaking as so much had gone into making ALEXCO a huge success. The Lord had so graciously blessed the company, both financially and with dedicated and faithful employees. It has been heartwarming over the years to hear the employees comment how wonderful it was working for a great company and such a wonderful family. But, in obedience to the Lord, we responded with a favorable reply to Kaiser. We knew He would take care of our people.

At the time of my writing this epilogue, it has been two months since I signed the letter of intent to sell. The process of due diligence and about 70 pages of legal work between our attorneys to develop an agreeable purchase agreement are now complete and the agreement has been signed. There are some minor issues yet to be resolved and the closing is expected to be completed before the end of the year. Kaiser has been very cooperative in structuring the purchase agreement to take care of the ALEXCO people, which I told them from the beginning was my greatest concern and their doing so would be required for me to sign the agreement. Because of ALEXCO's success, Kaiser has no plans to make any changes, and as a part of the purchase agreement they included employment contracts and favorable compensation packages for our management staff.

I have added this epilogue as some readers of this book may have an interest and check ALEXCO's web site. The decision to sell ALEXCO did not come without prayer, not only by the family, but also a faithful chain of prayer warriors that we are involved with from around the world.

Is there any significance in the Lord leading us to sell ALEXCO in these times in which we are now living? I can't answer that because I don't know. Though to sell the company was painful on one hand, it is also exciting on the other to walk in faith to see what the Lord will do next.

APPENDIX A

———

You can learn more about my brother's ministry in Kenya through my web site: www.bobfraleychristianlifeoutreach.com and clicking on *Help The World Direct* to see pictures of his ministry throughout the thirty years of his dedicated service in Africa.

If you are interested in donating to this outreach in Africa, you have our guarantee that every dollar you give goes to help those in need. We take nothing out for our expenses. All donations are tax deductible. If you would like more information, contact *Christian Life Outreach* either through their e-mail address xnlifeout@yahoo.com or call 1-866-998-4136.

CAMPAIGN SAVE
CHRISTIAN AMERICA

A sharp, focused "point of the arrow" message about America's unique and special place in world history and about what the future holds for our nation.

As you read this revelatory teaching, you will:

32-page booklet

- Learn about the very special and unique place that America holds in God's plan...
- Find out how to identify America in Bible prophecies dealing with the "End Times"
- Gain understanding into the incredible deterioration in moral standards that has overtaken our nation
- See the biblical answer to the spiritual warfare that is being waged over America
- Learn what YOU can do to address these issues and live in personal victory

A TIME FOR ACTION!
HOW TO PREPARE FOR WHAT'S AHEAD.

We are Living in the "Last Days." The American Christian has experienced the greatest level of spiritual warfare and defeat, in this last generation, than has been known since the founding of our country.

32-page booklet

We must understand that Christians are facing one of the greatest and most deceptive times of spiritual warfare that has ever been known. What can be done?

"A Time For Action, How To Prepare For What's Ahead", gives witness to what can be done to prepare yourself and your family to live in Spiritual victory and to "overcome" the attacks of the enemy. It will encourage you to take the first steps toward living in victory.

Both booklets are only $.40 each, minimum of 10 booklets.
25 or more booklets, $.30 each.

A Few Words from the Lord, Can Change Your Life Forever

**REALIZE THE
BLESSING OF OBEDIENCE**

Follow this remarkable true life story of how the Lord led two ordinary people for the saving of their family in these troubled prophetic times called The Last Days.

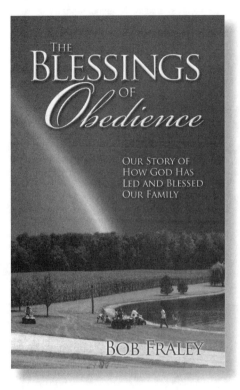

Many of the problems facing families today have been avoided by the Fraley family because God has honored and blessed their obedience. By their actions and choices, they have demonstrated (showing is always better than educational telling) what it means to live a life of faith and trust in God.

Their story is an inspiration and an example of what a person and a family can accomplish when God is at the center of everything they do and think. It is an inspirational model for us all—to be quiet and receptive to the God who speaks.

Today the Fraley family numbers 65 with children and spouses, grandchildren and spouses, great-grandchildren and continues to grow. They all, except those too young, serve the Lord even though each child has been active in school, the community and their jobs.

Published price $9.95
NOW $5.00 (S/H) for one book; $3.00 each (S/H) for 5 books or more.

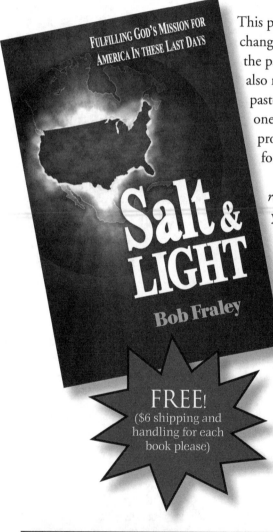

INCLUDES YOUR FREE INTRODUCTORY PACK FOR THE REMARKABLE REVELATION

Each starter pack has:

- A DVD of a half-hour television program with David Mains and Bob Fraley. This interview spells out a prophetic message God has laid on their hearts to help prepare His people for what's ahead, reviewing their new *50 Day Spiritual Adventure, The Remarkable Revelation.*

- Week One sample sermon

- Complete series outline matrix

- A promotional flyer

- A copy of both 32-page booklets:
  A Time For Action and
  *Campaign
  Save Christian
  America.*

GET YOUR FREE COPY OF BOTH OF THESE POWERFUL BOOKS TODAY

REALIZE THE BLESSING OF OBEDIENCE

Christian Life Outreach is only asking that you help by sending $8 per set to cover their postage cost and packing expense for each package. Along with each free book set, they are going to send you a free starter pack for *The Remarkable Revelation* teaching series based on Bob's book that is being used by churches across America.

FREE!
($8 shipping and handling for each set please)

INCLUDES YOUR FREE INTRODUCTORY PACK FOR THE REMARKABLE REVELATION

Each starter pack has:

- A DVD of a half-hour television program with David Mains and Bob Fraley. This interview spells out a prophetic message God has laid on their hearts to help prepare His people for what's ahead, reviewing their new *50 Day Spiritual Adventure, The Remarkable Revelation.*

- Week One sample sermon

- Complete series outline matrix

- A promotional flyer

- A copy of both 32-page booklets: *A Time For Action* and *Campaign Save Christian America.*

"THE REMARKABLE REVELATION: 50 Days to Prepare for What's Ahead"

GET YOUR ADVENTURE SERIES TODAY

Discover the answers to the questions about prophecy people are talking about:

- What does the Bible really say about America in the End Times?

- Why are so many popular ideas not found in Scripture?

- What will happen to the Church?

- How will spiritual warfare unfold in the last days?

The Bible tells us what to expect in the last days, but sometimes that message is obscured by tradition, popular entertainment, and teaching that is not grounded in the Word. *The Remarkable Revelation: 50 Days to Prepare for What's Ahead* is a series grounded in Scripture and easy to use for a church, a Bible study group, a Sunday school class or a family. The complete package includes a copy of *Salt & Light: Fulfilling God's Mission for America in These Last Days*, a copy of *The Day that Changed America*, a study journal, and a full array of series resources: 19 sermon manuscripts with Power Points, 14 man on the street sermon introductory interviews, nine short training sessions to help you teach this series, outlines, promotional materials, and much more.

www.bobfraleychristianlifeoutreach.com

- Use this package for your small group study or Sunday school class
- Use this package for your own family
- Use this study in your church

ORDER FORM:

| Quantity | Title | Each | Total |

SPECIAL OFFERS

____ Free copy of *The Blessings of Obedience* .... ea $5.00 S&H_____
5 or more copies .... ea $3.00 S&H_____

____ Free copy of *Salt & Light* plus the intro package to
The Remarkable Revelation .... ea $6.00 S&H_____

____ Free copy of both *Salt & Light* and *The Blessings of Obedience* plus the intro
package to *The Remarkable Revelation* .... ea $8.00 S&H_____

THE *Remarkable* REVELATION—
50 DAYS TO PREPARE FOR WHAT'S AHEAD

____ The Deluxe 2 DVD Package gives preachers and teachers everything needed
to unfold this series in your church or Bible Study .... ea $99.95 _____
plus Shipping and Handling ....ea $15.00 _____

SEPARATE ITEMS

____ *You Are Salt & Light, Equipping Christians for These Last Days*
(Study edition of *Salt & Light*) .... ea $12.95_____

____ *Campaign Save Christian America* booklet (minimum 10) ....ea .40 S&H_____
25 or more booklets ....ea .30 S&H_____

____ *A Time for Action* booklet (minimum 10).............................ea .40 S&H_____
25 or more booklets ....ea .30 S&H_____

S&H Prices are to cover Shipping and Handling.   Subtotal _____

CIRCLE PAYMENT METHOD: Total _____

Check   Visa   MasterCard   AmEx   Discover

Card #_____ Exp. Date _____Signature _____

Name _____

Address _____

City _____ State _____Zip _____

If your shipping address is different from your credit card address:

Name _____

Address _____

City _____ State _____Zip _____

Order online at www.bobfraleychristianlifeoutreach.com
Call Toll Free: 866-998-4136   Mail: Christian Life Outreach, PO Box 31129, Phoenix, AZ 85046-1129

www.bobfraleychristianlifeoutreach.com